Cat Butler

In the Service of Her Majesty the Pussycat

Bill Hall

First Edition, September 2009

Cover cartoon by Ty Wakefield

To order additional copies, please contact us.
BookSurge
www.booksurge.com
1-866-308-6235
orders@booksurge.com

For my wife Sharon who is at my side whenever life requires me to herd some cats

Table of Contents

1. Never stuff a cat through a closed door

Three cats hang around my house but that doesn't make me a cat owner. Nobody owns those hairy little deadbeats.

I am a cat butler. I assume the term is self-explanatory. But if not, a cat butler is a person who opens and closes doors for cats.

When the cat scratches on the outside of the door or calls out in its aristocratic fashion, you let it in.

When it goes to the door inside your home and repeats the command, you open the door and let it out. These actions usually take place seconds apart. A cat's favorite place is always the other side of the door—in and out, back and forth, with the butler opening and closing. They do it to flex their muscle—to prove who's the cat and who's the cat butler.

I know people who crawl out of bed in the middle of the night to let a cat in and out—eventually with the near hope that the little dictator will get hit by a truck. Go play in the street, Kitty.

I did that for years, letting cats in and out—eventually opening and closing the door in response to each command without even thinking about it, becoming an automatic door opener. It was my job.

And in truth, serving as a cat butler is preferable to the common alternative. The common alternative is called a litter box. Litter box is a euphemism for cat outhouse—except it isn't out; it's in. That's what's wrong with a cat outhouse. And unless you want a house that smells like an outhouse, you must take the disgusting contraption outside, empty it and refresh its sand—frequently. The damned things won't even flush.

We have retired the chamber pot from human use in this society in the interest of dignity and public health. But the cat chamber pot is still going strong, so to speak. Better a cat butler than a cat toilet attendant. Consequently, I have done my time letting cats in and out, out and in, ever the obedient servant, world without end. It's a demeaning existence and we wouldn't take it from anybody else. We don't even open the door any longer for women in this society, yet we open it for cats.

But no more. There is a better way. It is called a pet door. That is a clever little two-way flap that a child could install in 30 minutes, and I did it in five hours. You simply cut a hole in an outside door and install the device, complete with a kind of metal picture frame for neatness so you won't embarrass your cat with something tacky.

Next, you have to teach the cat how to use its little door. But that's not so difficult. It is accomplished by picking up the cat and repeatedly stuffing it, head first, through the door, first from the inside and then from the outside.

Make sure the screen door is removed or left open. Otherwise, when you are pushing the cat through from the inside, you will end up with a cat who has little waffle marks all over its face. That makes your cat cranky.

Pet doors are also used by dog owners—or, more accurately, by the dogs of dog owners. But pet doors are a danger to dogs. Pet doors come with a little square of plywood you can insert in them, blocking their use—turning the little flap a dog or a cat normally goes through into a sturdy little wall that neither a cat nor a dog can open. It is a useful device for those occasions when you want to keep your pet in or out.

But dogs, being more athletic than bright, never test the door first, the way a cat will. A cat will gently poke at the door with its paw, making certain it is open before easing through. Dogs are so enthusiastic and so strong that, the minute they hear their master come home, they dash through the pet door, whether it has the little plywood wall in place or not. More than one pet door has been ruined in that fashion. And more than one dog. That's why so many dogs have flat faces.

But pets are not the only ones who go through pet doors. So do pet owners. My sister-in-law had an oversized pet door installed for her kitty. She pampers her pet and was determined to ease its journey through life and through the door. She installed the large cocker-spaniel-sized door to give kitty a wide berth so the poor pussy wouldn't bruise its whiskers on the way in and out.

My sister-in-law is the absent-minded sort who is always forgetting her keys. So she is constantly grateful that she has a larger door. About once a week, she gets down on her hands and knees in her power clothes and crawls through the pet door, presenting one of the family's best aspects to the world in the process.

Pets are quick to learn how to use their little doors. Our cats figured it out in about a week. (My sister-in-law got the hang of the cocker-spaniel door in about 12 hours.)

Our cats learned so quickly because it was winter and we customarily feed the cats inside. We simply stuffed them out the door and they were so anxious to get back in where the food and warmth was that they started patting at the flap. The next thing you knew, they were opening their little door and entering the house. They had become cat butlers.

However, they were far less inclined to go outside. They would sit in front of the door, occasionally patting at the flap and kind of peering out. And then they would sit there some more. It is my theory that a cat, of all people, hates to pop out of a hole into the gaping jaws of God-knows-what because a cat has spent its life as the gaping jaws, waiting at the edge of a hole for the furry little morsels that pop into view. Going out a cat door is a mouse-like thing to do and therefore unnerving to a cat.

But cats get over that for the most part if you keep stuffing them through the hole, and especially if you remember to open the screen door. Once they overcome the fear of being mistaken for a big mouse, they relish their freedom. They can come and go as they please, even when the human cat butlers aren't around. It liberates the cat as well as the cat butlers.

However, there is a catch. There is always a catch with a cat. They can let themselves in no matter what their condition, no matter what they have with them. And they'll drag in anything they can get their claws into—birds, mice, unwary Avon Ladies. I hate it when they drag an Avon Lady through the little door. That riles Avon Ladies. They won't stop bellowing until you buy at least a case of avocado eye shadow.

Worse, the other day I found a little pile of feathers and bird bones on the floor by the bed—the crumbs, so to speak, from a feline fast-food dinner.

There was nothing to do but go get the vacuum and clean up the leftovers. I knew what the cat was thinking as it smugly watched me vacuum:

Once a cat butler, always a cat butler.

2. Why Bossy People Hate Cats, And Vice Versa

"I don't like cats," a newspaper editor said to me one day with that characteristic gift management people have for belaboring the obvious. "They're so unmanageable."

Of course, they're unmanageable. That's what normal people like about them.

That's what management types hate about cats: they're mavericks. They won't keep their place. Cats are to pethood what feminists are to sexism. They'd rather rip your face off than stoop and grovel.

So of course, the little rebels aren't manageable. That's the whole point of a cat, the whole reason it was created.

There isn't much doubt a study would demonstrate that executives—managers—are the people most likely to find cats offensive.

And vice versa.

I'll bet the study would show that most managers prefer dogs. A person can order a dog about. You can tell it what to do. A dog is manageable.

Indeed, a dog is a born serf, a willing doormat, an eager, emotional wimp. A dog will rush forward and lick your hand the minute you enter a room. That's what executives like about dogs. Executives don't find that kind of conduct strange or embarrassing. Executives wonder why the people who work for them don't do that more often. Managers adore a heartfelt slobber.

In fact, when you get right down to it, managers don't mind an utterly insincere slobber. A slobber is a slobber. That's why managers prefer dogs to cats.

I'll bet King George III loved servile dogs and hated cats because, spiritually, cats were the first signers of the Declaration of Independence.

On the other hand, the foolish Founding Fathers of America were enamored of the notion that independence and freedom are the natural state of humankind.

Not so. Humans, like dogs, are natural serfs. That's why dogs are fond of humans and vice versa. Basically dogs like to worship masters. So do most humans. It is invariably a minority, not a majority, that opposes each new despot. There were more Tories—"Oh, for goodness sake, let's not offend a sweet man like the King"—than rebels in the New Land.

Similarly, dogs—"I just love my master, even when he kicks me"—don't do democracy well.

Cats are the most American of all animals, including human Americans. They aren't going to take any crap off anybody. They are born rebels. There wouldn't be a dictatorship left on earth if cats were more numerous. If you had a country full of cats and some clown tried to take over, the cats would dig a hole and bury him.

There are other animals, besides cats, who won't do what you tell them. But that doesn't necessarily make them rebels. Being unmanageable can also be a sign of having fur for brains. And managers always assume that anyone who won't follow orders—whether a cat or a person—doesn't have a lot upstairs.

As a matter of fact, you could make a case for that. For instance, you don't look down at a night crawler and say, "Roll over, boy."

If you did, the night crawler wouldn't roll over. A night crawler is a few bricks short. A night crawler doesn't know roll over from the Funky Chicken.

Similarly, you don't throw a stick out in front of a chicken and yell, "Fetch!"

A chicken will just cock its head and blink at you if you do. A chicken will just cock its head and blink at you whatever you do, even if you approach it with malice and a cleaver.

And if you say to an ant, "Sit up, boy, sit up!" an ant won't sit up, not in a million years.

This is not because an ant is independent or democratically stubborn. It is because an ant is about as vague as you would expect of someone who eats beetle parts and runs around the neighborhood with a tiny rock in its mouth. A cat would never do that.

The dog may be man's best friend but it is also the least American of all animals in its passion for servile relationships. A dog loves a dictatorship, a master, a manager. If a dog doesn't have a despot to direct its life, it will adopt one, rushing up to the first stranger it encounters and volunteering as a fawning, groveling, fuzzy serf.

And let's face it, dogs have no judgment about the dictators they choose. They will accept and serve for life any leader, no matter how cruel or inept. Dogs are a lot like Afghanistan's Taliban in that respect.

A cat doesn't refuse orders like an ant, merely because it doesn't understand a bloody word of what it is being told. It understands only too well. A cat refuses orders because it will not condescend to follow orders. And if you have to ask why, then you think like a dog and neither the cat nor I can explain it.

Cats are undiscriminating in their refusal to be managed. They refuse any direction from anyone, no matter how kind or competent the cat butler. They won't take orders, even in their own interest and as a matter of survival. When the chips are down, they are utterly unmanageable. They are a lot like the Founding Fathers in that respect.

3. Jealousy And The Green-Eyed Cat

If your spouse nonchalantly brought home a new lover one day and sat there in front of you each night watching television while blatantly stroking the intruder on all the favorite stroking places, what would you do?

You would consider the house much too crowded is what you would do.

You would decide the welcome mat had been withdrawn is what you would do.

You would hit the road is what you would do.

That's what Sterling did when Sheldon arrived. And small wonder. It should hardly be surprising that your first cat gets bent out of shape when you bring another cat into the home.

And don't give me that malarkey that adding a new cat is the same as bringing a new brother or sister into the house. Some cats will buy that line. But not most Siamese cats.

True, some cats won't mind. Some cats are promiscuous. Some cats are real alley cats in that respect. But Siamese cats tend to be monogamous. And by God, they expect you to be the same.

Consider Sterling, for instance. Sterling is a characteristically cross-eyed Siamese who gets even more cross-eyed if he has to share you with anyone. In fact, if he has to share, he gets real squinty-eyed and mean-looking.

He is named Sterling because we value him highly. To us, he is a precious commodity. He is also named Sterling because, when we took him in, he was silver colored. The silver tarnished. As he matured, he grew darker and darker.

In mood as well as in color. He almost left the house for good before the crisis had run its course. But it was partly his own fault. That's because a Siamese tends to be a one-person cat.

Me, for instance. In a choice between me and my wife, he always showed a rather open preference for me. I don't know why. Maybe it's because I have fur on my face and she doesn't.

Oh, he was always friendly enough to her. He did the usual for a one-person cat. Each time he entered the room, he would tour the occupants, stopping to give everyone a friendly nuzzle, including my wife.

But then he would come to me and settle in. He would snuggle up and fall asleep next to me. I guess I'm kind of comfy.

My wife was not oblivious to the meaning. She had seen the same behavior with people. A person will enter a room, shake a hand here, pat a shoulder there, maybe peck a cheek or two and even give an old friend a chaste hug.

But a person will customarily sleep with the one person in the room he truly loves, not with everybody at the party (though we have all known colorful exceptions to that rule).

Not that my wife was jealous. She knew there was no alienation of affection involved, no hanky panky. She knows, when the chips are down and the lights are low, that I escort Sterling from the bedroom and sleep with her.

Granted, Sterling would get a tad crotchety each night as he was shown the door of the bedroom. He would get a little more cross-eyed than usual. But he must understand that he and I are merely dear friends and his crankiness is nothing compared with what I would be in for were I to ask my wife to leave the bedroom each night so that she didn't disturb the cat.

Besides, a thing like that can tend to come out in a divorce and be misunderstood entirely.

And the truth, whether Sterling likes it or not, is that I met my wife first and I wouldn't choose him over her even if she weren't a better snuggler.

For her part, my wife has kept the whole thing in perspective. She understands that a Siamese needs to attach itself to one member of the family, perhaps not so much for reasons of affection as for reasons of establishing some normalcy in one's comfort. A person doesn't like a different pillow to sleep on each night and a Siamese doesn't like a different person to sleep on each evening in front of the television set.

I'm sure Sterling would be the first to want it plainly on the record that it is no insult to my wife that he found her too bumpy and lumpy to sleep on. After all, what a man would regard as an attribute in a woman cats regard as a drawback in a pillow.

But my wife was lonely. She also wanted a snoring fur comforter in her lap while we watched television. And our other cat, old Delilah, was no comfort. She was usually off under the bed. (Sterling never minded her. She was there when he arrived. And he seemed to regard her as what she was—an old maiden aunt.)

My wife wanted a lap cat, too. So she found Sheldon, a cream and black Balinese with a tail like a monkey, fur like a rabbit, a pink nose and, oddly enough, prominent pink lips in the center of his dark face. The pink lips give Sheldon an eerie resemblance to Al Jolson in blackface. And maybe that had something to do with Sterling's negative reaction. Sterling is mostly black now. He may have mistaken this new Al-Jolson-blackface cat for some kind of sick racist joke.

Whatever the reason, Sterling practically vanished from the first day Sheldon arrived. Jealousy was plainly a large part of it. As far as Sterling was concerned, my wife had been unfaithful. So had I.

He would accept none of the blame himself. Oh, sure, he had tilted more toward me than toward her. But he felt he had been faithful in his fashion to her and to me jointly. And he didn't need to remind her that he was a steady part of only one menage a trois, whereas she and I had just formed a second arrangement.

And if he had tilted toward me at times, so what? Everybody has to tilt some way. But she should know that she was also his person.

For all the good it did him.

All of a sudden, she walks in with that pink-lipped little bastard and announced that it was her cat.

Her cat? What had he been?

And as for me, I seemed to be going along with it. Oh, sure, I still tilted toward him but I was also friendly to the pink-lipped little bastard. What a pair of dog-breathed turncoats.

So he split. Even though it was winter, he would vanish for a day or two at a time, returning only occasionally to visit the only loves he had left—the food dish and the heat vent. And if either my wife or I tried to reach out a hand to pet him, he would run away. He gave us a shoulder colder than the winter.

But little Sheldon was happy. And he proved, like many cats, to be rather promiscuous. He was quick to cuddle with anybody he bumped into, including me, the mailman, the meter reader, the Avon Lady, a terrified dachshund down the street, any sincere tree and all of our visitors, pleasant or unpleasant. He just threw himself at all of them. It was pretty embarrassing.

If the shoe had been on the other paw, Sheldon wouldn't have minded in the least. If we had been linked with Sheldon first and had then brought Sterling into the house, Sheldon wouldn't have batted a blue eye. Easy Sheldon throws himself at everybody in sight and he expects his humans to do the same.

But my wife was concerned about Sterling. So we got out a book to read up on Siamese cats. And there it was in print: the book said Siamese often do not take kindly to new arrivals in the household and will sometimes even go away and never return.

Given the benefit of hindsight, I can see how amazing it must have been to Sterling that we looked up what was wrong with him. From his perspective, it was our behavior that was abnormal.

Things are better now. Sterling is starting to stop by my wife for a pat now and then. I think he's beginning to forgive her. And it doesn't hurt a thing that he and Sheldon have found they like each other. On a good day, Sterling lets Sheldon wash his face.

Meanwhile, I have tried to be more sensitive. I do not shun Sheldon. When I come home, I tour the room, patting a shoulder here, shaking a paw there, but nothing intimate. And then I settle down with Sterling, falling asleep with him on the couch.

But I still show him the way to the bedroom door when my wife is feeling frisky. I don't care what Sterling says, I like lumpy and bumpy.

4. The Woman Who Dressed Cats

The cheerful dingbat on television was stuffing a large cat into a tiny dress and she assured her viewers that cats just adore being dressed in human clothes.

The eyes of the cat said otherwise. If the woman had given him half a chance, he would have ripped her throat out.

"It's a big lie that cat's don't like to wear clothes," she said, as she stuffed another paw through a sleeve and the cat glared at the camera, hating the dress, the woman and all humankind.

"You love to dress up, don't you, sweetie?" the lady cooed, tying a little bonnet with a bill on it under the cat's angry, trembling chin. His eyes, full of raw, unvarnished hatred, peered out from beneath the bill of the bonnet like two hot coals in the dark. If looks could kill, that woman was dead meat.

There was a reason the woman on television was so anxious to convince people that cats like to be dressed in little people clothes. She runs a shop selling little people clothes for cats. She has a vested interest in making us think cats are just dying to dress like we do.

She's full of it, of course. The eyes of that cat prove she's full of it. But common sense tells us the same thing. Cats don't like to be dressed because they are already dressed. It is only we who are required, in the interests of modesty and warmth, to wear some false fur.

A cat is already wearing his clothes. He wears them all over his body, even on his face. And when an animal goes to the length of clothing his face, he certainly doesn't need the frilly trappings of some cat boutique. Lord knows, an animal with clothes on his face has already gone above and beyond the call.

And if you think a little dress is redundant on a cat, how about a fur coat? The lady with the cat place was actually selling fur coats for cats. Can you imagine one animal wearing the pelt of another animal? There are few creatures savage enough to do that and cats aren't one of them.

The fact is, cats hate any fur but their own. Indeed, on those cold days when our cats bring a mouse through the cat door for a warm breakfast inside, they spit out the fur. They leave little fluffs of mouse hair all over one corner of the house. They chew the mouse but they eschew the fur.

It is similar to the way a teen-ager eats pizza. Teen-agers love pizza but they hate pizza crumbs. They eat the pizza and spit the pizza crumbs out on the carpet, just like a cat eschewing mouse fur. I know. I find mouse fur and pizza crumbs on the carpet in front of the television set all the time.

(Oddly enough, a cat will sometimes come along and eat the pizza crumbs but a teen-ager will never eat the mouse fur. Mouse fur is one of the few things a teen-ager won't eat.)

The things we do to our cats. For instance, I know a woman who vacuums her cat. She uses one of those hand-held, cordless, rechargeable vacuums and she swears her cat loves it. It helps the cat get rid of its loose hair. Apparently the cat goes along with it in the belief that vacuuming cuts down on hairballs.

We tried the vacuum on Sterling, our middle cat—our hand-held, cordless, rechargeable Siamese. He ran over in the corner and sat glaring at us like we had tried to put clothes on him.

Why do people do that? Why do they constantly try to make animals into little people, dressing them, talking to them, giving them food with people-food names like Beef Banquet? We do that to cats, to dogs, to horses, to my strange Uncle Chester—to any kind of animal, trying to make them human.

It's the bowler-jogger-Christian-vegetarian-Republican syndrome. Bowlers and joggers and Christians and vegetarians and Republicans and all the other fanatics aren't content to practice their passion by themselves and let it go at that. They have to drag everybody else into it. Converting others to your hobby, religion or politics is some kind of self-flattery, some imagined affirmation that you are superior because everyone is joining your side.

Similarly, it isn't good enough for us that a cat is a cat. We have to make it into a little human, to prove that being human is better than being a cat.

In the first place, I never had any doubt. I would hate to be a cat, eating raw creatures, fighting in the alley, breeding in the bushes, depending on patronizing humans for my sustenance, being stuffed into dresses by cheerful dingbats.

In the second place, cats don't agree that being human is better than being a cat. They prefer being cats, the fools. They don't like being little humans.

And they're right. Cats make lousy people. A cat as a cat can be a handsome creature. But a cat can't cut it as a human. A cat in a dress makes a sinfully ugly human being—a shriveled gnome with hair all over its face, crooked legs and even a tail, for God's sake. I look ugly in a dress and my legs are less hairy than a cat's.

If people insist on putting cats in dresses, they should at least shave their legs.

5. The Human Cat Breast

Have you ever been treated like a breast?

Of course, you have, whether you have the nerve to admit it or not. Anyone who has ever spent any time next to a contented cat has been treated like a breast. Anyone who has sat next to a cat has been pumped like a cat boob by two furry little feet.

This is not because the cat has actually mistaken you for a breast. Few of us resemble cat hooters in the slightest. And we can all be tremendously grateful for that. No, a cat doesn't do that disgusting thing it does because it has you confused with the faucets on its own kind. The fact is that a cat who begins pumping you like a milk bladder and purring its hairy little heart out is simply helpless to do otherwise. It is a conditioned reflex.

When a cat was a kitten, it was never more content than when it was dining at Mom's warm table. The more it pumped that breast, the faster dinner was served and the greater the contentment. A memory like that sticks with a cat deep into its dotage. Consequently, whenever a kitty is content with the milk of human kindness, it must pump something.

You, for instance—whether you look much like a cat breast or not. And I'm sure you don't.

When you push a cat's contentment button, its automatic pump begins. And it pumps whatever is within reach, no matter how mortifying the target may be to you personally—your thigh, your fleshy arm, your plump, breast-like little paunch, even your flabby face if you let those frenzied feet within reach. You get near a contented cat and you're going to get pumped like crazy, you boob.

Frankly, that's a mixed blessing at best. On the one hand, it is no small honor to be declared an official substitute cat chest for an evening. There are lesser distinctions in this life than to be declared so extraordinarily heart-warming by a cat that it involuntarily begins responding to you with the same loving motions it once used on dear old Mom.

On the other hand, I don't know about your own personal weirdness but I am not altogether at ease playing the role of a cat hooter.

But who are we to be so proud? Sure, cats run around treating people like breasts. And sure, you and I would never do anything like that, except at the most unusual parties (and then only for charity). Nonetheless, we are similarly afflicted with our own embarrassing habits ingrained in our personality during our early time at breast or bottle. We, too, spend our lives doing foolish things stemming from that very same suckling instinct.

Smoking cigarettes, for instance.

Slurping on a chaw of tobacco, for yucko-instance. A cat might regard half the world as one big, pumpable breast but it wouldn't stuff its face full of snoose.

Boozing, for instance.

Gorging on potato chips, for instance. And on peanuts and Twinkies and Cracker Jacks and brownies and chocolate chip cookies.

We all pump a boob in our fashion. We nibble. We munch. We gnaw and chew. We spend our lives keeping that old nipple nibbler working for all it's worth because, like a cat, we simply can't overcome the urge.

And sure, when a cat begins pumping away at your plump underside, it can be a little embarrassing, especially if the queen has popped in for tea—or worse, one of the macho dudes from your softball team. The queen, resplendent with a regal chest of her own, can understand such matters. Softball players are not often so sensitive.

It can be distressing to get worked over by a cat when company comes to call because there is no hiding the fact a cat is treating you like a breast right there in public. You wish the little pervert would take up smoking instead, or at least mouse nibbling.

But you needn't be so smug. When the cat sees you smoking or sipping or nibbling, it immediately recognizes the suckling impulse you are answering. It knows how kinky your conduct is for an allegedly mature adult. That's why, when you've got the old nipple gnawers working at a cigarette or a beer or a sack of chips, the cat has one of its chronic looks of disgust on its kisser.

That's why I won't nibble on chocolate chip cookies if there's cat watching.

But sometimes, when the urge for cookies is overpowering, and I'm truly contented, I will push my paws against the cat.

6. Putting A Cat In Neutral

I'd advise you to behave yourself around my wife if you know what's good for you.

I know three cats who didn't behave themselves around her and it altered their lives—as well as their whoopee glands.

Delilah, our tabby, had started showing some signs that she was hankering to have six or eight litters of kittens each year.

My wife had Delilah's tubes tied.

Then Sterling, our eldest male, started tangling in the alley with other hotheads. And he began to christen the furniture.

My wife took him in and had the vet shuck his walnuts.

Next Sterling and Delilah started shredding the couch.

My wife had them declawed.

When we acquired young Sheldon, it wasn't long before he began spritzing and shredding the furniture—when he wasn't fighting.

My wife had him trimmed fore and aft.

I witnessed all of that and, I assure you, I show a lot of respect for the furniture. And I never fight, especially with my wife.

They say you shouldn't identify with a pet when having it fixed. And I don't especially. I try to remember that the critters are probably better off in the long term if they are no longer inflamed with the same furies that send male humans out in the alley behind the beer bar to joust with bare knuckles over some woman. In fact, not only can you make an argument that brawling cats would be healthier and happier with their glands adjusted but probably so would the kind of human males who habitually end up out in the alley behind the beer bar. I certainly know what would have happened to such men at our house if they persisted in their scuffles—especially if they damaged the furniture in the process.

Nonetheless, I admit it does give a frisky person a twinge to be one of the co-conspirators in stifling the sexual urge in a cat, even if it does improve their lives overall, even if it lengthens their lives. For one thing, I'm sure the loss is greater with some cats than with others. Cats are undoubtedly like people in that some are a good deal more easily overheated than others. Sexually, the two kinds of people in the world are not men and women. And they are not heterosexual and homosexual. They are the horny ones and the not-so-horny ones. There are people, male and female, with a strong sex drive. And there are people, male and female, who yawn a lot over the subject. The widespread belief of prior times that men were the frisky ones and women the not-so-frisky ones is an idea as dead as the cajones of a fixed cat.

(I'll never understand why they call it fixing a cat when they break it. That is a euphemism worthy of the Defense Department. If you were to actually fix a cat, you would give it a testicle transplant. So let's be done with this doublespeak and say bluntly what was done to the cats: my wife had them broken.)

I confess I have never been part of that half of human-ity that yawns over sex. But I feel perfectly moral because I am always respectful of the furniture. And let's be candid about this: a lot of people who are indifferent to sex are nonetheless rough on their furniture.

I'll admit that it does give me pause when I am in-volved in the medical procedure that ends forever a cat's participation in the ancient social custom of looking into another pair of eyes and asking, "Your place or mine." It is troubling that, because of me, a cat will never again spot someone special across a crowded alley.

Or at least if he does, he won't care. When a neutered cat says, "Frankly my dear, I don't give a damn," that is pre-cisely what he means.

I recently learned to hate being involved in the castra-tion of a cat for another reason: It isn't easy to drive across town to the vet with a cat climbing up and down your head because he has reason to believe he is about to lose his jewels.

It happened one day when we learned that young Sheldon had developed a lump on his side. Of course, the first thing you think of with a cat is an abscess. Our cats get abscesses about every 15 minutes. When that happens, we summon Doctor Florence Housecall who is the good news and the bad. She is the good news because calling at your house for minor vet chores saves you money.

She is the bad news because one of the ways you save money is to become the official cat holder while she deals with the ailment. When some strange woman is poking at a cat's tender wound with a sharp object, the cat has a tendency to try to shred the flesh off the arms of the official cat holder.

For good measure, a frightened cat releases much of its hair. I guess it's a defense mechanism, a way of leaving an attacker with a mouthful of fur while the cat who was once attached to that fur gets away.

I understand that. Shortly after I grew up, I looked at the world through clear eyes for the first time and became so frightened that most of the follicles on my head let go.

But whatever the reason a frightened cat does what it does, it does it in wads. And you can always tell the official cat holder from the cat after an abscess treatment. The official cat holder is the one with cat hair all over his body.

But this time Doctor Housecall decided the problem was a hernia. I guess Sheldon had been lifting heavy mice. It would require a trip to a pet hospital for an operation. While Sheldon was under, my wife wanted to deal with his rude relationship with the furniture, especially the spritzing. It would be an opportune time to have the cat neutered. (Neutered is a more accurate term than fixed. When a cat is neutered, it gets stuck permanently in neutral.)

It would also be a handy time to have him declawed. We didn't mention the declawed part to Doctor Housecall because she has declared declawing "mutilation" and opposes it. We consider a shredded couch mutilation.

I gather there is some debate in the vet community over how disabling it is to declaw a cat. Suffice it to say that they only remove the front claws, whereas a cat's prime defense is its back claws. For good measure, declawed cats continue to climb trees. And the ghastly truth is that a declawed cat will go right on catching birds, mice, slow lizards and occasional Avon Ladies—and bringing them into the house through the cat door for the cat butler to deal with.

But there is an inconsistency among those vets who discourage declawing. The same vets who discourage declawing encourage castration. I, for one, would rather lose my fingernails.

But Sheldon was destined to get the works. And my wife had already played official cat holder earlier that day so that meant I had to be the one to take the cat to the hospital. My wife was still too fuzzy to drive.

It was on that day that I learned the virtue of placing a cat in a box or in a cage of some sort while piloting it down the road. We had been on the way about 20 seconds when Sheldon began freaking out. He raced around the car, jumping into the back seat, then onto the back of my neck, up onto my head, and then over onto the dashboard and back around the circuit for another trip.

And all the while he was releasing hair like crazy, including some of mine as he leaped from the top of my head to the dashboard.

This all took place while I was trying to drive. But they couldn't have got me for inattentive driving. I have never been more attentive in my life. There is something about waiting for a cat to jump on your head that makes you attentive as the devil.

I suppose it was the sound of the car engine. Sheldon hadn't been in a car since he was a kitten.

Or was it more than that? Animals sometimes sense these things. They get nervous before an earthquake, for instance. So it wouldn't be amazing if they could also sense when their dating days are about to end, when the earth will move no more.

And for that matter, was he actually freaking out as he romped across my head time and time again? Or was he punishing a traitor to his sex?

I don't know. I'm just grateful that when they put me in the hospital a few years ago for a hernia operation, I escaped with my fingernails.

7. Three Kinds Of Bigot

Have you ever noticed that it is the dumbest men who consider themselves superior to women?

And that it is the worst examples of the white race who consider themselves superior to black people?

You never see a male Nobel Prize winner who thinks that men are superior to women or that white men are superior to everyone. It is rednecks with an I.Q. of 14 who believe they are superior. And it is the dregs of the male sex who look down on women.

Have you ever noticed that?

And have you ever noticed that most of the people who hate cats are people who own dogs?

8. Lips In The Night

There is nothing that will chill your soul faster than to awaken in the dark of night to the sound of animal lips smacking.

I have finally learned that it is merely Delilah, our old tabby, but it can set your teeth on edge until you figure it out. Delilah is simply one of those cats with a wet mouth. She has some overabundance of spit. A lot of people are that way—kind of slurpy and loose lipped, always spritzing you when they get excited and talk too fast, the sort of people you don't like around when you are eating but who come in handy when you have a lot of letters to mail.

Delilah is like that. There are times when you wish she would go away, like when she crawls up behind you on the back of the couch and drools on your neck.

On the other hand, having a lot of spit can be an asset for a cat. Needless to say, she is our cleanest cat.

I think it's Pavlovian. You remember Pavlov. Every time he fed his dog, he rang a bell. Before long, all he had to do was ring the bell and the dog's chops would start dripping saliva.

It is less well known that, after a time, the dog took to ringing the bell, which filled Pavlov with an irresistible urge to feed the dog.

Television pet food commercials work on us in somewhat the same way.

Similarly, Delilah's wet mouth stems from some such conditioning, except that she has gone overboard. Somewhat like Pavlov's dog, she associates pleasure with saliva—but not just when food is involved. She gets drippy whenever she is happy for any reason, but especially when she is sitting on the back of the couch above your neck.

I am proud to say this cat is almost always dripping like a cheap roof. That's how happy we have made her. If we made her any happier, she would expire of dehydration.

As it is, we live with a series of wet trails through the house. At times, it looks like we have a giant snail for a pet. Delilah is the wettest animal I have ever known and I once kept tropical fish.

Delilah is never happier than when she has sneaked into the bedroom for the night and is sleeping on my feet. When she sees us stirring around, getting ready to turn in for the night, she hides under one corner of the bed, waiting until lights out and we are asleep to sneak out from under the bed and back up on my feet. And there she stays until the middle of the night when I awaken with wet feet and evict her.

We have given her a hard time over this rather rude habit. On the one hand, we might not mind having a kitty keeping us company for the night. On the other hand, not this kitty, not this feline monsoon. Sleep comes hard enough for a writer without trying to sleep with wet feet. And so each night before turning in, we try to remember to get down on our hands and knees and check for the moist cat under the bed.

She's usually there. But when you reach for her, she moves just beyond your grasp. That brings on the broom. We use the broom to poke at her until she finally capitulates and races out of the room.

That got to be a chore—until I discovered something: Each time I fetched the broom, I would bounce it, bristle-first, off the floor half a dozen times before getting down on my hands and knees and poking at her with it. Before long, she got the message. Soon all I had to do was bounce the broom on the floor and she would race out from under the bed and toward the door.

We had conditioned her. First there was Pavlov's bell. Now there is Bill's broom. It is the same process.

Nonetheless, each time I use the broom, it makes Delilah furious. I can tell. Her mouth stops dripping.

There are still nights when I forget and she hides under the bed. But the broom has changed her ways. She now knows better than to crawl up on the bed after I am asleep and start dripping on my feet. She stays under the bed.

But for her, even that is enough. Even that gives her pleasure. She is ecstatic to be spending the night with her crotchety humans. So she begins drooling.

And dripping.

And slurping.

And smacking her lips.

That's what I wake up to in the still of the night—that eerie smack, smack, smack of what is obviously an animal, an animal of indeterminate size.

I tell you, there is something in the marrow of our bones that does not like the sound of an animal salivating somewhere in the nearby darkness.

Every time I hear that midnight sound, my mouth goes dry.

❖　❖　❖

9. Never Overestimate The Brains Of A Cat

Let's stop kidding ourselves and be honest about it: Cats aren't as bright as we like to pretend they are.

Oh, they're not especially dumb as animals go. They're smarter than mice and a good deal brighter than some birds and they could best a block of concrete in an I.Q. test nine times out of ten.

And they are easily conditioned, just as we are, to the benefits to be enjoyed from reciprocating affection.

But smart they ain't. If you want to get technical about it, they are even dumber than dogs and that is world-class dumb.

I can explain why some people think dogs are intelligent. The only people who think dogs are intelligent are dog lovers. And even dogs are smarter than dog lovers, virtually by definition. A dog can be as dumb as a dead stump and a dog lover will still consider the poor, pathetic fool a genius.

But no moderately intelligent person considers a dog smart because a dog does have the virtue of an utterly honest face. A dog looks as dumb as it is, if you're smart enough to see it.

A cat looks a lot smarter than it is. Indeed, a cat looks downright wise.

A dog gives away the game. It runs yippy-yapping all over the place, tongue hanging out like a politician in season, panting frantically and looking honestly idiotic. Most people who run around with their tongues hanging out are untidy in mind as well as in mouth and a dog is certainly no exception.

Cats do their frantic panting on the inside. They are a tad slow themselves but at least they have the few brains required to keep up appearances.

And because they don't run yippy-yapping all over the place, because they are calm, they create the illusion of wisdom.

We have all known people like that. They sit around sedately and all crinkly eyed, blinking occasionally like Confucius and, most important of all, not saying much. Such people are often considered profoundly wise. People who say little are widely regarded as thoughtful, when the truth may be that they are merely too slow to keep up with the conversation. They say little because they have so little to say.

Nonetheless, it is amazing—and instructive—how frequently silence is equated with wisdom.

Cats benefit from that misconception. They are routinely regarded by their admirers as bright. And without all of that panting and leaping about so common to dogs and to freshmen members of the state legislature, who is to know the difference?

That's why some cat owners may be a little brighter than dog owners. Anybody with any brains need only look at a dog to see it for the witless wonder that it is.

A cat, on the other hand, does wear the mask of intelligence and can fool some of the people some of the time. But the truth is that the I.Q. of the average cat is five.

That's not quite as embarrassing as it sounds because most cats are lousy at geography and it skews their test scores. They probably deserve at least a seven.

Nonetheless, cats carry off the illusion of brains so effectively that people will talk to them. A person will look his cat in the eye and jabber at it like it has a full head of brains.

And if the cat doesn't fall asleep and if it blinks wisely, then the cat owner immediately assumes the creature has understood the entire conversation.

It hasn't. It has detected some pleasantness in your manner.

It has recognized a cordial posture and tone.

It has acknowledged, as a conditioned reflex, the presence of a loyal cat butler.

It blinks, it yawns and it may even utter a small meow. This modest response is immediately mistaken for conversation, for a coherent gesture on the part of the cat.

It isn't. And it doesn't change the fact that the I.Q. of the average cat is five (or seven for the few who can manage geography). A snort or a grunt does not constitute affirmation of a thought being communicated. Ask any married couple.

A cat's occasional meow in apparent response to human conversation is nothing more than a cat's way of grunting. A meow is to a cat what a grunt is to a husband who is being talked to by his wife while he watches bowling on television. It doesn't even remotely resemble intelligent conversation.

(Husbands watching bowling on television have an average I.Q. of nine.)

10. Grandkittens

How come grandchildren are so popular and grandkittens aren't?

People are anxious—even insistent—that their grown children produce grandchildren. But the same people are anxious—even insistent—that their grown cats avoid producing grandkittens.

There is a reason:

When cats start producing grandkittens, they get carried away. They overdo. They go nuts. When it comes to having kittens, cats have never heard of the words moderation or self-control or keeping your fur zipped.

A person wouldn't mind grandkittens if a cat would simply show a little restraint, if a cat had one kitten every 14 years or so. But the frisky little devils can't seem to contain themselves. Or at least, they can't stop containing kittens. Cats are more like grapes than like people. They reproduce in bunches. Once they get their kitten-producer churning, they can't seem to turn it off. Cats are repetitious.

A lot of modern young people are somewhat the opposite. A lot of them get wrapped up in their silly careers and keep putting off the principal obligation of their lives— to make their parents grandparents.

However, in fairness to modern young people, parents give their children contradictory moral advice in these matters. They spend the first 20 years or so of a daughter's life admonishing her to keep her shorts on—and the years after that nagging her to get in the sack and crank out some grandchildren. They spend her early life shooing away teen-age boys in heat and her early adult years asking her when she's ever going to get it in gear. They beg her to be careful and then they beg her to get reckless.

You don't have to beg a cat to get reckless. I gather there is nothing a cat would rather do than get reckless.

We humans show some moderation in our child bearing, especially now that science has given us the means. Once your daughter gets her kid-producer started, she has the means to turn it off from time to time. She won't crank out more than three or four kids as a general rule, and rarely more than 18.

A cat can bang out 18 in a year.

That's overdoing it. That's taking a wonderful thing like motherhood and twisting it into a shameless fetish.

But we often intercede. We have them altered. Even Catholics have their cats altered. A Catholic might not be able to understand how there could be such a thing as too many people on earth. But it takes only a couple of litters of kittens before a Catholic or anyone else can grasp the concept that there is such a thing as too many cats in one house.

Nonetheless, it is troubling to dwell on the fact that we are constantly pushing our married children to have kids while we have seen to it that our cats will never be parents. However, cats need to understand that there is such a thing as self-control. A person can't simply sit by and watch the house fill up with kittens. If a cat won't get its glands under control, then a person is forced, in self-defense, to deal with those glands medically.

After all, it's the only way to prevent littering.

11. May You Bury Your Cats

"May your children bury you," is the melancholy Irish blessing. And that's a charming, not an ugly, thing to say. It doesn't mean, "I hope your kids get a chance to bury you soon."

It means, "I hope you live to a ripe, old age, but, with God's mercy, you will die before your offspring do and thus you will never know the pain of burying a child."

It is not so terrible in the scheme of things for a child to bury an aged parent. But when a parent buries a child, it reverses the natural order and fractures the continuity of a family. Nonetheless, there was once a time, not so many years ago, when people who had children fully expected to lose some of them. It went with the territory of starting a family.

These last few decades have been the first in the history of the world when people in the wealthier and healthier countries could reasonably expect to be outlived by all their children. The combination of smaller families and vastly improved medicine means that most of us in this nation will never know the horror of burying a child.

But in much of the world today the remarkable thing is that people start families with the almost certain knowledge that there will be some funerals along the way. And the same was once true in this country.

I stopped at a small family cemetery along the road in southern Utah a few years ago and there in that overgrown plot were the headstones of a mother and six children, all lost to the 1918 influenza epidemic. The smaller children died first, one by one, over a period of weeks. And when the last small child was gone, the mother and the eldest, a girl of 14, died—both within hours of each other. The mother and the eldest daughter had clung to life, dragging themselves from bed to bed, nursing the young ones, trying to save them. And when that cause was lost, when they had exhausted the last reserves of strength and devotion, the mother and elder daughter wilted and died.

Few families were hit so hard during that epidemic or at any other time. Nonetheless, that Utah family is a reminder of the countless generations before this century began when most families had their share of small graves. Rearing those customarily large broods in a time before antibiotics and other miracles involved accepting the loss of a child or two during the course of your life. Parenthood meant, not just sniffles and cuts and occasional broken arms, as it does now. Parenthood meant a few premature funerals along the way.

The only thing remotely comparable most of us have today is pet ownership which involves, not merely some losses, but the loss of virtually all the pets you attach yourself to in the course of your life. For most people, the tie is not as close with cats as with children. But it is close. You miss them when you lose them.

Over a lifetime, a cat owner can go through a dozen or more of the critters. You bring a Sterling, a Delilah or a Sheldon into your home with the understanding, and the expectation, that you will grow attached to your new pet—

and that you will lose it. You accept future pain when you accept a cat. It's a play-now-cry-later proposition.

But in another sense, that's not so awful. As short as a cat's life is, better to outlive a cat than to be outlived by one. Indeed, a selfish part of you will fervently hope that you will one day lose the cat—that you will live long enough to do so. Sterling, Delilah and Sheldon may have somewhat the opposite hope, but if you're 50 and the cat is five, you can't be blamed for preferring that he beat you to the finish line.

The difference between cats and kids is that it is a blessing to say, "May your children bury you."

But it is a rather nasty shot to say, "May you be buried by your cats."

12. `Just Call Me Kitty`

All cats are named Kitty.

You might as well accept that. It doesn't matter what you name them. If it isn't Kitty, they won't come when you call.

You can name a cat Nancy or Noodle or Herman or Fluffy or Mouse Breath and you can call that name until your brain breaks and nothing will happen.

But no matter what handle you hang on a cat, you can step to the door and yell, "Here, Kitty, Kitty, Kitty!" and Kitty will come.

Some of the time.

If he feels like it.

All cats are named Kitty. Similarly, all colonels are named Colonel, all priests are named Father and all doctors are named Doctor. That's handy. You don't have to remember their real names. You could go to a cocktail party of cats, colonels, priests and doctors and not embarrass yourself by forgetting someone's name.

"Why of course, I remember you, Kitty. Isn't it a lovely party?"

But just because cats, in their opinion, are all named Kitty doesn't mean that you shouldn't give your cat an additional name. It helps tell them apart in conversation. Not only that, but calling your cats Abscess and Hairball is more charming than resorting to such simplifications as the little cat and the gray one.

But names can shape your cat. Oh, they don't shape him the way names shape humans. We tend to become what we are named. I know. My given name is Wilbert. That is a silly name. I became silly. But what would I have become had I been named Bruno or Fang or even Abscess or Hairball? Names like that can color a person's life. They tend to be self-fulfilling prophesies. A man named Gwendolyn is less likely to become a pro football player than a man named Beefy. And who would be more fun at a party, a woman named Chastity or a woman named Whoopee?

You probably can't have quite the same effect in naming a cat or we would all name our cats Cleans-His-Own-Litter-Box. But you can color the personality of a human or of a cat by what you expect of him. You treat someone like an incompetent and he's likely to live up to that judgment. You treat him as reliable and he's likely to prove you right. Hence your attitude has some bearing on how a cat turns out and the name you choose defines your expectations.

So never name a cat Craps-All-Over-The-House. It is likely to make you too tolerant of the fact he does so. In a more modest vein, names like Lazy, Crabby, Filthy, Dumbo and Barfer also tend to promote an atmosphere that guides a cat in the wrong direction.

But if you have already made the mistake of giving your cat a name that has degraded his personality, it is not too late to change it. The cat won't mind. He knows his real name is Kitty anyway. He'll humor any new inaccuracy you care to devise.

I change the names of our cats from time to time. For instance, I sometimes call Delilah by the new name of Sparky. It's a dog's name. From time to time, I appoint her our honorary dog because we don't have a dog any more. Declaring one of our cats a dog is the best way there is to have a dog without all the usual inconvenience and noise.

Besides, the name fits in this case because Sparky is dumb enough to be a dog. And everybody should have a dog, especially if it doesn't behave like a dog.

Sparky doesn't behave like a dog. Sparky doesn't even behave like a cat. Sparky sleeps under the bed 23 hours a day, coming out for a few minutes now and then to eat. Most of the time, Sparky behaves like a dog in a coma and that's the best kind of dog, even if she is a cat.

Fortunately, Sparky is unlike a regular dog in another way: She doesn't shout. Dogs shout. A dog never speaks except at full volume. It's like having some deaf old uncle living in your house who shouts every word he speaks.

"IS DINNER READY YET?"

"IT SURE LOOKS LIKE RAIN!"

"THE PRICE OF BEER WENT UP AGAIN!"

"I'M AGAINST SILENT PRAYER IN THE SCHOOLS!"

"IF DINNER ISN'T READY YET, WHEN IN THE HELL IS DINNER GOING TO BE READY?"

Dogs are like that, always bellowing, especially about dinner. Their volume knobs are stuck on high.

Cats don't shout. They swear a lot, but usually under their breath. And they do screech a little during war and sex, but who doesn't? At least they don't shout at the top of their lungs during ordinary conversation the way deaf uncles and dogs do.

I wonder if dogs are deaf.

Sparky is the best dog of all—a quiet dog. And it's all achieved by the miracle of how you name your cat.

You also have to admire the tradition of some Indian tribes who let the facts name their children. They wait to give them a permanent name until their personality emerges. If the child is clever, they name him Little Coyote. If he is graceful and hard-working, they name him Dancing Beaver. If the kid turns out to be a real little son of a bitch, they name him Crooked White Lawyer.

We should show the same patience in naming a cat. We should wait to see which of a cat's many untidy habits will suggest the appropriate name.

But let's be realistic: What you name a cat and what the cat's name is are two different things. Cats call each other Kitty, just as doctors call each other Doctor. It is a way doctors have of establishing a brotherhood and setting themselves apart from the riffraff.

When you want to call a cat, you don't step to the door and yell, "Here, Barfer, Barfer, Barfer!" You yell, "Kitty, Kitty, Kitty!" even though you have named the cat Barfer.

Similarly, while strolling the halls of a hospital, you hear, "Doctor Affluent to Emergency." You don't hear, "Melvin to Emergency."

That doesn't mean there aren't other ways to call a cat. The best way is to use the sound of food being served. Anyone who owns a cat and an electric can opener knows that cats are quickly conditioned. They quickly learn that they hear that sound every time they are fed. Before long, they come running every time they hear that sound whether they are being fed or not. And there's nothing that is more likely to make a cat stomp away swearing under its breath than to hear that magic sound and run out into the kitchen to witness the opening of a can of boiled okra.

But they are so greedy, so constantly famished, that they will fall for it every time. That is useful. If you need to summon the cat for some other purpose—a little trip to the vet, for instance—stick the electric can opener out the window and grind away for a few seconds. In this modern age, it is no longer the tweet of the bird or the squeak of the mouse that summons a cat. Today it is the call of the can opener.

We shifted to dry cat food a few years ago but we are still able to call the cats. The hard nuggets of dry food rattle into the plastic dish with a sound that brings the cats running.

And they say you can't train cats.

All cats are named Kitty. But when it comes to dinner sounds, they should all be named Pushover.

13. Cupboard Love

It's called cupboard love. When Sheldon—sometimes a bit standoffish toward me—begins rubbing against the backs of my legs at dinner time, caressing my calves with his hairy sides, that's cupboard love.

It's the kind of bogus affection a person shows you when he wants something. Telling a woman you love her just to get into her knickers is cupboard love.

The used car salesman who fawns all over you while you consider buying one of his hopeless heaps is exhibiting a form of cupboard love.

People who suddenly become religious again and start praying when one engine quits on the plane are demonstrating a common form of cupboard love.

And of course, cupboard love is what politicians do for a living.

But the most common form of all is the kitty version, the cat who won't give you the time of day between meals but who makes love to your legs every time you get near the cupboard where you keep the cat food.

Which raises the eternal question: Do our cats love us or do they love our cupboards?

It's an ignorant question, just like most either-or propositions about human beings. Are people nice to you because they are nice? Or are they nice to you because they want to sell you something?

The answer is both. Some people are nice because they are nice and some are nice because they want something. Cats are the same way. Some of them rub all over you because they adore you. Some rub all over you because they want another helping of Carp Stroganoff.

And if the truth be known, some probably rub all over you for the semi-selfish reason that they get their jollies from rubbing all over people, the little perverts.

But some cats are shameless people users, fuzzy little tramps who won't molest your leg unless there's a meal in it. They are gold diggers. But you can get carried away with that judgment. Even a gold digger will sometimes develop some genuine affection for the old fool she is taking advantage of.

And so the person who tells you that all cats are independent—that they merely use people without offering any real affection in return—is not very perceptive. People who say that all cats are manipulative are usually the sort of stiff, cold-legged people that no cat would want to molest.

In most cases, affectionate cats show affection largely to receptive people—weird people who enjoy having their legs molested. But you can't generalize. There are also cheap, easy cats like Delilah, constantly starved for affection, willing to do anything for a seedy thrill, who will throw themselves at the first leg that comes along, no matter how unfriendly.

At the other extreme, there are cold, calculating, little people users, emotionally empty cats who wouldn't give Mother Teresa the time of day if she didn't have a meal they could mooch.

Cats, like people, come in all varieties. Some of them are nice because they are nice. Some are nice because they want to get in your cupboard drawers.

Which raises another question:

When I snuggle up to my wife, is it because I love her or is it because I want something?

Both. It can be both. Cupboard love doesn't mean that you don't love the keeper of the cupboard as much as you love the cupboard's contents.

14. We're All Cat Couches

How come a cat likes to sit on your chest and breathe mouse fumes in your face?

Our other friends don't do that. Nor do our relatives.

Oh, it's true that Aunt Mildred used to hold me on her knee and breathe muscatel in my face. But she stopped that when I was about 27. And she never sat on my chest, for which I am immensely grateful.

But a cat will sit on your chest and breathe mouse fumes in your face. There's something about a cat that makes it miserable if it isn't right up in your face.

And they're sneaky about it. If you stretch out on the couch, cats will crawl up on your tummy. And that's all right. A cat on your tummy can be quite comfy.

But then they start creeping up, trying to get a little closer to your face.

And closer.

And closer, until they are lying there on your chest with their nose next to yours, breathing mouse fumes in your face.

But it's not the fumes I mind so much, or even a wet nose next to mine. I can handle that. And it's a bit of a stand-off anyway. If the cat doesn't mind a little espresso breath once in a while, then who am I to complain?

But it is unnerving to try to relate to somebody who has his face that close to yours. We simply don't do things that way. When you sit around the house with family and friends, you keep a little space between you and them. You don't go nose to nose with them while you're talking to them. It makes your eyes cross.

And you can't see a person's whole face when it's so close. I like to be able to see a person's whole face when I'm talking to him and not just his forehead or his nose or his left eyebrow.

Or his fuzzy little chin. I like to see all of a cat's face when I'm lying on the couch with him, and when he is lying on me, using me as a couch.

I'm not comfortable around a cat who is so close to me that he's out of focus. That's too intimate. I don't like to be that intimate with somebody who never brushes his teeth and who showers by spitting all over himself.

So I try to break a cat of sitting on my chest and breathing in my face. I have always tried to discourage anyone from doing that. If a person can't sit on a chair like a lady and keep her face to herself, I don't want anything to do with her. Or with a cat of the same manners until he learns to back off a bit and sit on my stomach and breathe on my chest.

I have learned several ways to make a cat back off. One way is to blow in its face. That makes cats all squinty-eyed and angry. But it drives them back where they belong.

Or, each time a cat creeps up into your face and begins sharing its revolting breath with you, jump up suddenly and dump its furry fanny on the floor. You do that a few times and it gets the message. Anyone would.

But why do cats want to stick their faces into yours anyway? You would think they would have learned long ago to knock it off because they have got themselves in a lot of trouble over the years by doing that. The old belief that a cat sitting on a baby's chest was trying to suck the breath out of the baby brought a lot of cats to an untimely end. You would think they would have wised up by now.

However, I'm sure it's a compliment when a cat tries to mash its face into yours. When cats get together among themselves, you see them sitting there nose to nose, softly breathing warm breath on one another. It's just a thing that cats do when they're friendly with each other. It's kind of a disgusting thing for them to do, but perhaps little different in its fashion from a bunch of people sitting around together smoking stogies or chewing tobacco or drinking buttermilk. And if a person must choose, I'd rather sit and talk to someone with mouse on his breath than buttermilk.

But the fact cats normally sit around breathing on each other at point-blank range is no excuse for their sitting on my chest and doing the same to me. After all, cats don't sit on each other's chests.

They owe us the same consideration. When they treat us like common couches, we have the right to object, the right to fight back. When a cat sits on you and exhales in your face, you are within your rights to blow in its face or to jump up and dump it on its furry fanny.

And if that doesn't work, try sitting on the cat's chest and breathing in its face for a while. That'll usually straighten them out, especially if you have been drinking buttermilk.

15. The Grandfather Who Refused To Beg

I was always more fond of my grandfather than I was of my cats. Some might consider that strange because my grandfather used to puff on a smelly old pipe and most of the cats I have known never did.

And I didn't prefer my grandfather to cats simply because he was a better story teller and at least as agreeable a companion. Nor was it because he bounced me on his knee, which the lousy cats refuse to do.

I think the one thing that set my grandfather more apart from cats than anything else was that he didn't get up early and beg for food at the door each morning, the way a lot of cats and grandfathers do.

My grandfather did get up early. It goes with age. The older we get, the earlier we tend to rise. I don't know why that is. I suppose it has something to do with the feeling that the fewer the days remaining to you, the more you want to see them all the way through.

It's an odd thing but we spend our working days trying to drag ourselves out of bed at 7 in the morning. And yet when we retire and can finally sleep in, we start rising at 6:30 and then at 6 and before long, at 5. Talk about living our lives backwards.

Consider teen-agers, for instance. No one is more difficult to rouse in the morning. Yet it is teen-agers we send off to school at some ungodly hour. And it is our elders, who don't want to sleep in, who are free to sleep as late as they like.

Why not the other way around? Our elders get bored with nothing to do but eat bran flakes and listen to repetitious cable news. They would relish rising early and going off to high school. The very thought of it would make them young again. And if there is anyone who would enjoy retirement, it is teen-agers. Most of them are already retired—every moment you let them. They would be a lot better at retirement than our elders are and a lot more willing to do it. And no one could make better use of a chance to sleep in than a teen-ager. Retirement is wasted on the elderly.

I have no idea what my grandfather was like when he was a teen-ager—probably the same as I was, willing to sleep till noon if anyone would let him. But in his final years, he became a typical retired person, which is to say, like a cat.

Cats and senior citizens are daytime dozers. So are teen-agers, if the subject is mathematics or history instead of sex and music. Teen-agers are full of energy only when you are talking about sex and music. If the subject is mathematics or history, teen-agers are senior citizens. They drift off. They nap a bit.

Like a cat. Cats are alleged to be nocturnal. That's a lie spread by cats. How do we know it's true that they work at night? We're usually asleep at night when cats are supposed to be out roaming, doing whatever their job is in the middle of the night. (I think their job in the middle of the night is sex and music, just like teen-agers.)

But they don't do their job all that often. I have frequently seen cats asleep in the middle of the night. Indeed, many a cat has slept on me in the middle of the night. I suspect the truth is that cats sleep day and night most of the time. Occasionally one of them will be stricken uncharacteristically with a little touch of insomnia and wander out at night. Some drunk coming home from a party will see it and swear that cats are up and about during the wee hours.

Mostly they aren't. Cats are born retired. They doze a lot. They are awake for approximately 20 minutes a day on the average. They awaken briefly at 5 in the morning when they come to the bedroom door and start raising hell about breakfast.

Unlike my grandfather. The older he got, the earlier he rose each morning. I don't know why. Maybe he didn't want to miss the last bus to high school. Whatever the reason, my grandfather awakened at 6:30 and, after a few years, at 6. And then at 5:30. And so on, until near the end of his life, he began rising at 4.

But unlike the cats, he didn't go to the bedroom door of my aunt and uncle, with whom he was living, and make a ruckus about breakfast. Unlike a couple of cats I could mention, he was too much of a gentleman.

And when my aunt finally awakened a couple of hours later and walked out into the living room, she would find my grandfather, sitting there calmly smoking his smelly pipe and listening to his stomach rumble, but without complaint.

Unlike cats. When their stomach starts growling, they join in.

My grandfather is long since gone. He now sleeps the clock around. And sometimes I think the cats call out each morning, not only for food, but to remind me of the grandfather who used to sit alone with his smelly pipe in the middle of the night wondering what the cats now wonder:

When is one of those shiftless, overgrown teen-agers finally going to climb out of bed and fix breakfast?

16. Pink Nose

How would you like to be looking in a child-rearing book and run across a notation that your kid has a lousy nose?

That's what happened to us. We were looking at a cat-rearing book under Balinese, the race of our youngest, Sheldon, and under "faults," it listed "albino nose." Sheldon has an albino nose but it isn't his fault. It isn't anybody's fault. It isn't a fault at all. It is, like nearly all declarations of superiority and inferiority in physical appearance, an arbitrary declaration, not a fact.

It's like my nose, which is also albino, or at least white, and which also happens to be pointy. White noses are acceptable, indeed even superior, in some circles. But needle noses are regarded as faults, along with huge noses, bulbous noses and crooked noses. Somewhere there is a people-rearers book and, under "faults," it lists needle noses.

Says who? Where was I when they voted? Where were black people when they took the ignorant vote those many centuries ago on which is the best color and which is a fault? Where were the people with allegedly wrong noses—who constitute a majority—when the vote was taken on which nose is the correct one? We've got to do a better job in the future of getting our people out to the polls.

These are all arbitrary, irrational designations. Somewhere back in some vague pocket of time, some collection of jerks got together and declared what makes a great face and what doesn't. They chose their own characteristics, of course.

They could as easily have been a different collection of jerks and declared it to be needle noses that are blessed. Then it would be all the people with those little turned-up, Miss America noses who are the flawed ones. And it would be all the needle-nosed people who are hailed as the cute little stunners.

Along with albino-nosed cats. If the right people had been in charge of declaring what constitutes perfection in Balinese cats, instead of these albinophobes, it could be pink-nosed Balinese who are the fancy ones and the black-nosed ones who come in last at cat shows.

After all, there is something kind of original about a black face with a pink nose in the middle of it, kind of a built-in beauty mark, kind of like rounding up all of your freckles and getting them together in one spectacular location.

Fault? Appearance isn't a fault. And it isn't a flaw or a mistake. People wouldn't refuse me a job, saying, "I'm sorry but you made a mistake with that nose."

But as we speak, there is some collection of twits somewhere, sitting around voting, without letting you or me know that the polls are open, and they are pointing at a cat with a pink nose and saying, "Get that little freak out of here. That nose is a fault."

And it isn't just cat-judging twits. It is movie director twits and artist twits and model agency twits and assorted other twits throughout the centuries who have given us our almost universal conception of what is beautiful and what is not. And like a bunch of pliable twits, we go right along with it. I sit there watching television with my pointy nose on my face, looking at someone with a "perfect" nose and saying, "Boy, is she a knockout. And what a terrific little honker she has."

And her nose certainly is beautiful. But so is mine. And so is yours. I'm the head twit on this election and I hereby declare the polls open. All those in favor of declaring all noses beautiful, raise your right hand.

No, no, your right hand. Left hands are wrong.

17. The People Breeders

Cats can make or break a marriage and they do so deliberately.

Cats know that people who go to bed happy are more likely to make more people.

Cats know that couples who go to bed angry are less likely to procreate.

If a man and wife are cat butlers, the sort of obedient people who pamper their cats—feeding them, caressing them, spoiling them—a cat wants more people like that on Earth. So he tries to get them in a loving mood, a breeding mood. He tries to lighten their lives.

When they've had a tense day at the office, he becomes affectionate. He snuggles and purrs and rubs up against them. It's hard to stay tense with a hairy vibrator rubbing all over you.

When his owners come home worn and blue, he gets comical, racing around the house, chasing his tail, pouncing on a puff of dust. When they're feeling low, he goes into his silly cat act. He makes them laugh.

So they go to bed without their cares. And when they go to bed without their cares, they are more likely to manufacture more people like themselves. They are more likely to crank out obedient cat butlers.

But sometimes a cat is owned by an indifferent couple who forget to feed him, people who yell at him, people who ignore him while they lavish incomprehensible affection on some insipid dog. When a cat ends up with people like that, he is, of course, determined to see that Nature does not reproduce their kind.

He causes trouble. If they come home tired and cranky, he aggravates the situation. He knocks the lamp off the table, causing an argument over whose cat it really is and who should have to clean up the mess.

If they start acting affectionately toward each other, the cat sneaks into the bedroom, smears lipstick on one of the husband's collars and leaves the shirt on the bed where the wife can find it.

When a cat engages in that level of sabotage, his owners are less likely to go to bed compatible. They are less likely to repeat Nature's mistake and produce more crabs who don't pamper their cats.

We may breed cats to suit our fancy but cats consider the practice a two-way street. That's why there are more and more people around making fools of themselves over cats. The fuzzy people-raisers have installed that tendency in our genes through selective breeding.

But what if you're a couple beyond the age of producing babies?

Cats, for all their instinctive cleverness, are too dumb to know that. So all you have to do is pamper your cats and they'll find a way to get you in the sack anyway. Treat them right and they'll make a habit of keeping you happy and ready for love.

The fact is that cats give you an incentive to treat them kindly even when you're past the point of procreation.

Maybe they're not so dumb after all.

18. Lousing Up A Great Hobby

When I go into a pet store and see all those cages of listless animals and the harried store owners standing there, I feel sorry for them—the store owners, I mean.

I feel sorry for them because I presume they entered the business as cat lovers or dog lovers or even bullfrog lovers. I presume they decided to get into the business because they thought they would enjoy the work—and its little beady-eyed companions—more than they would enjoy the money it might return.

That's like deciding you enjoy your grandchildren so much that you go into the business of selling them to strangers.

Worse, opening a pet store is turning a perfectly pleasant hobby like cat ownership into a business. How many people have done that? They take something they love to do—like making candles or cooking or sleeping with sailors—and they ruin it by turning pro.

If you convert a perfectly pleasant hobby into a profession, the next thing you know, making candles or cooking or sleeping with sailors is suddenly work. As soon as you turn fun into something you have to do, instead of something you love to do, you get to the point in no time at all where making candles, casseroles or sailors is drudgery.

The people who open pet stores are little different. They didn't realize at first the difference between caring for a couple of animals at home for love, and cleaning the cages each day of 1,200 cats, dogs, birds and tarantulas for money.

People who open pet stores never stop to think beforehand that it takes far larger reserves of love to see you through the feeding and changing of 25 garter snakes and 14 albino ferrets than it does to see you through the care and cuddling of your own household kitten.

It is not the same thing to tidy up the rug of one's own home after an accident-prone cocker spaniel who regards you as a god as it is to change the litter under dull-eyed colonies of fat gerbils who will soon be delivered for your financial gain into the strangling fists of lethally clumsy little humans.

If people must open pet stores, they should open pet stores that specialize only in animals they don't much care for. Cat lovers should sell dogs and dog lovers should sell cats.

A cat lover could learn to relish selling dogs.

Especially the neighbor's dog.

19. The Vastly Overrated Cat Honker

If a cat ever gets down on its hairy knees and thanks the Almighty for anything, it should be for the fact that a mouse is even dumber than a cat. A cat on its own would starve to death if mice weren't so dumb.

I was watching our smartest cat with a mouse the other day. And to say that Sterling is the smartest of our three cats is to use a relative term. But I don't mean that the cats are relatives. I mean that one of them is smart strictly by comparison with the others and not by comparison with a stump.

Sterling has fur for brains the same as any other cat. But at least he has thick fur for brains. By cat standards, he is a genius. By comparison with Delilah, he is Phi Beta Catta.

I have known and lived with Delilah in close quarters for four years now and she still forgets from time to time who I am. Nine times out of ten, she recognizes me. But then suddenly, I will come home, and she will patter forward, sniffing the air a bit and sit in front of me, staring up at me with her head tilted sideways wearing a puzzled look on her little cat kisser. She gets this who-the-hell-is-that look on her face.

I am her father, that's who. I am her adopted father. She sees me daily—morning and night; I hardly ever travel. And yet every 10 days or so she forgets who I am. Every 10 days or so she examines me with a quizzical look that says, "That face rings a bell, but I can't come up with the name."

And so I get out a little cat food. And I freshen the water in her dish. And then, slowly, like a state legislator trying to understand poverty, it comes to her. A little look of recognition dawns. You see the thought cross her alleged mind:

"Oh, yeah, it's one of the cat butlers, the one with the furry face."

Sterling isn't anywhere near that dumb. He always recognizes me. But that doesn't mean he's ready to enter a chess tournament. Oh, as cat's go, he's a cut above average. He probably has a couple of I.Q. points more than a contestant on "The Price is Right." But no more than that. We're talking cat here, not Einstein.

But by comparison with a mouse, we're talking Einstein and then some.

You should have seen what happened the other day. I arrived home to find Sterling out on the lawn where he had caught—or, more probably, tripped over—a mouse. And that's always kind of a sad scene, a scene that leaves you sort of torn, especially when the mouse is very much alive, as, unfortunately, they often are with a well-fed cat.

On the one hand, a certain parental pride wells up in you that a cat of yours has succeeded in the hunt—or in the stumble, as the case may be. It's as if your 12-year-old son has gone forth into the city on his own for the first time and brought back a Big Mac that he hunted down and killed with his own hand. Sure, you feel a little sorry for the Big Mac but after all, the forest is full of them. And more to the point, today your son became a man. So tough luck to the Big Mac.

Unfortunately, a mouse is considerably more appealing than a Big Mac. I always forget how tiny they are, no bigger than your thumb. And they have fur all over them, just like a real animal, just like a pony or a bunny or a doggie or Uncle Chester before the gin killed his follicles. The mouse is twitching this way and that, like some toy that Walt Disney invented. And in its fear, its soft, furry, little sides are heaving as it pants in terror.

Fortunately, our own food is not so inconsiderate. Our own food is dead and gone. No problems of conscience arise in consuming a steak or a drumstick. (The rumor that a drumstick was once the leg of a bird is a vicious lie.) The only live food consumed by humans is that eaten by vegetarians who have no ethics when it comes to pulling delicate, terrified little things up by their roots and stuffing them into their fat vegetarian faces, oblivious to the tiny vegetable screams.

Cats are like vegetarians. They like to torment a thing before they stuff it into their mouths.

Indeed, most domesticated cats aren't all that interested in eating a mouse. And who can blame them? It's not terribly appealing. A cruel vegetarian might bite the bottom off a live carrot but cats won't ordinarily do that to a mouse. Cats simply like to worry a mouse a bit. And that was what was going on the other day as I arrived home.

Sterling was out on the lawn where he had this mouse cornered. And the odd thing was that the poor little creature would occasionally escape. But not far because mice are even more vague than cats. Sterling would look the other way for a moment and the mouse would creep away a few inches.

But only a few inches. Being a mouse, with seeds for brains, it moved off in the grass six or eight inches away from Sterling and blithely assumed it was safe.

It was almost correct. Sterling looked all around, including straight at the mouse, and never noticed. Nor did he smell it. I don't know where in the world cats ever got a reputation for a keen sense of smell. You can put a reeking piece of rotted liver directly under a cat's nose and the cat will never find it if you don't put your finger on it and show him where it is.

And sometimes not even that will do it. Sometimes you have to grab the cat by the back of the neck and cram its nose into the rotted liver. If you do that, they'll find it two times out of three.

But when it comes to sniffing out rotted liver on its own, a cat can't cut it. Somewhere along the evolutionary line, a cat's sniffer crapped out.

And so a mouse has all the chance in the world to escape. You would think, with the cat sitting there looking puzzled and with his sniffer extinct, that a mouse would simply make a break for it.

But it doesn't. It toddles on a few steps and thinks that takes care of the problem.

And half the time it does because a cat will never notice.

But what was really mortifying the other day was when Sterling was searching about for the mouse, he finally gave up and then sat right down on it without the slightest idea of where it had disappeared to.

And the mouse probably didn't understand where the cat was either. The mouse probably thought it had found its way to a safe haven beneath a fur-covered rock.

It is not an easy thing to see your own cat sitting ignominiously on a mouse and wondering where it went. How would you like it if your 12-year-old brought home his first Big Mac and then couldn't find it because he was sitting on it? I don't mind telling you I was pretty embarrassed. After all, I am Sterling's father.

And Delilah's when she recognizes me.

20. How To Rile A Senior Citizen

Medical science is frequently full of it but perhaps never more so than in its contention that cats calm the elderly.

How can that be when no one knows cats better than those who have lived for decades at the beck and call of those officious little troublemakers? The longer you live, the more dead birds, mice and small dogs you have been called upon to remove from atop the doorstep and from beneath the bed where the cat has dragged them.

The longer you have lived, the more hairballs, cat accidents and mangled mice you have dealt with. It is the elderly who know cats best of all. And yet medical science would still have us believe that cats have a calming influence on the elderly.

Specifically, it is said that cats are useful in a nursing home, partly because petting a cat will lower the petter's blood pressure—and also the blood pressure of the cat.

In one sense, I can believe that. Some people carry so-called worry stones with them. A worry stone is an uncommonly smooth, satin-finished stone. Rolling it around in your hand, stroking a sensuous surface with the tender tips of your fingers, has a calming influence. You can achieve the same effect by patting the soft, naked bottom of the one you love, though the habit is generally discouraged in public, which is why people substitute worry stones for bottoms when out on the street.

A cat can serve the same function as worry stones and worry bottoms. Researchers insist that if you place a cat in the lap of nursing home patients and suggest that they pet its soft fur, it will calm them—providing it is not too large and vicious a cat.

Stroking a cat brings back memories of those other soft scenes from our lives—a mother's arms about you, a lover's touch, the cool hand of a kind nurse on a fevered brow, the gentle grasp of a doctor's huge, warm hand as he accepts the latest check from Medicare.

Ours is a life of gentle and soft, of warm and furry, of fuzzy feelings and loving touches. So there is some link for an older person between touching soft, furry objects and the calming memories of life. But a cat does stretch the theory to the limits.

You spend your life picking up and wiping up after a cat, opening doors and closing them, feeding and watering, waking up to their first shrill command of the day, trying to sleep through their melancholy love songs. You spend your days and nights as a cat butler and then, at life's close, you are finally liberated from their bondage. And so it is hard to believe that you could bring a pain in the neck like a cat into the presence of someone gratefully liberated from such chores and not produce aged shrieks of horror.

There are trials in this life we must endure, not the least of which is sloppy pets and drunken relatives. And one of the blessings of growing older is that you can sometimes be emancipated from such trials. So you wouldn't expect people to be grateful if you were to bring some loud, drunken uncle back into their lives long past a time when they thought they were rid of the old windbag. You wouldn't walk into the nursing home and say to one of the patients, "Here's Uncle Chester come back to live with you." You wouldn't say a thing like that and expect to lower anybody's blood pressure.

And after all my years of living the life of a cat butler, if you were to plop some tattered tabby into my lap, my blood pressure would go through the roof. When a person grows older, he should have to do neither windows nor hairballs.

On the other hand, there are probably days at the close of life when even some old reprobate of an uncle would not be automatically unwelcome. Even a few familiar worries are like old friends when you're bored. And perhaps most welcome of all would be the reminders of life as it was, warts and all.

Some nursing homes do better than others in these matters. Some pay more attention to maintaining the familiar aspects of former lives. Just because muscles have retired and you now dribble in your jeans doesn't mean that you don't still enjoy a cup of coffee and a friendly conversation. The better managed nursing homes keep the coffee pot on.

And just because you don't go to an office every day doesn't mean that you don't still love to gather with a few cronies at 5 o'clock and lighten the day with a cold glass of beer. Thoughtful nursing homes have little cocktail hours.

And just because your spouse is gone and your chicks have flown and your friends await you on the other side doesn't mean that you wouldn't be cheered to see a creature that, for better and for worse, was a regular part of your life—whether that is Uncle Chester or that damned cat.

They say that elderly occupants of nursing homes who have gone months or even years without uttering a word will often end their silence if you suddenly bring cats and kittens back into their lives.

And maybe that's why they say that petting a cat will lower the blood pressure of the person who pets it. And the blood pressure of the cat. Sometimes cats don't have much use for us either but they're suckers for a gentle old hand.

So, yes, I believe it gladdens the heart of an elderly person if the management of a nursing home is kind enough and wise enough to give a couple of cats the run of the place. After all, those places are served by squads of nurses and attendants. It would lower my blood pressure, too, if I knew I could sit on the porch, petting a kitty, secure in the knowledge that others would be cleaning up the hairballs.

21. Roast Of Robin

Why don't cat food manufacturers sell canned mice and birds? Why don't they cater to cats instead of to cat owners?

Why do they sell beef for cats? You never see a housecat go out on the range and kill a cow. And if I ever did, I would never sleep again under the same roof with that cat.

Cows are people food. Why don't they sell cat food to cats? Why don't they sell canned sparrow tidbits?

Why do they sell pork to cats? You have never in your life seen a housecat wrestle a pig to the ground and have it for breakfast. Housecats are too tidy to wrestle a pig.

Pigs are people food. Why do they sell it to cats? Cats like bugs. Why don't they offer little packets of dried grasshoppers for cats?

We feed hay to horses. We feed bird seed to birds. (But don't try to plant it and grow a bird. Bird seed is actually plant seed.) Why don't we feed cat food to cats?

Well, of course, you know why the stores cater to us by offering the food that we like instead of the food cats like. We have money; cats are broke.

Contrary to popular opinion, cat food manufacturers aren't in that business because they are interested in pleasing cats. Cat food manufacturers are in that business to please themselves, to make money. They will make more money if they pander to people palates and ignore what cats like.

But it serves cats right that they don't have any money. The day the lazy bums stop sleeping the clock around and go out and get a real job is the day they will start seeing canned mouse on the shelf. They have only themselves to blame.

That's why all the cat food you see at the store is more appetizing to people than to cats. It is purchased by people and people don't buy food that sounds good to bankrupt cats. Cat owners buy cat food that sounds good to them. They should call it cat-owner food because it certainly isn't cat food.

This explains why cats must exist on a lot of mashed slop and dry crud that they don't like instead of getting the flavors they really want—bugs, birds and mice. Actually what cats are compelled to eat is something worse than bugs, birds and mice. Even people, if they knew what was in those cat food cans, would prefer bugs, birds and mice to the actual contents. Oh, sure, the can labels say things like beef, pork, chicken and fish. But they don't say which parts of the beef, pork, chicken and fish. And let's face it, they don't exactly use the center cuts of the meat. They don't use the breast of the chicken. They don't use the choice portions of the fish. The prime portions of the beef, the pork and the fish are sold to people for human dinners.

They also sell people the best parts of the chicken but, in addition, they sell us some of the weirder parts of the chicken, mashing them together to form breaded chicken chunks for sale at fast food restaurants patronized by heedless teen-agers with dormant palates. Actually, you can feed a teen-ager pretty much the same trash you feed a dog because neither dogs nor teen-agers chew. They gulp.

The food barely grazes their tastebuds. A teen-ager will eat shredded newspapers providing you mash it into a patty, deep fry it and pour catsup over it.

In truth, a cat is only a little more discriminating. A cat would prefer mouse to beef but a cat will take whatever it's handed rather than get a job. Humans, by contrast, want food for their cats that appeals to human sensibilities. That's why the manufacturers don't come straight out with which parts of the cow, pig, chicken or fish are to be found in those cans and sacks. We don't want to know. But deep down, you know which parts:

It's the eyebrows, nose and ankles of the cow. And worse.

It's the eyelids, nipples and snout of the pig. And worse.

Its' the tails, fins and gills of the fish. And worse.

It's the lips, ears and nostrils of the chicken. And there is nothing worse than a chicken nostril.

If cat owners fully realized that, they would probably prefer that their cats eat bugs, birds and mice. In fact, if they knew what is in some mashed chicken sandwiches at the fast food restaurant and in some canned sandwich stuff made of "meat products," they would probably prefer bugs, birds and mice for themselves.

But they don't know. The cat food manufacturers hide the odd animal parts and the parts of odd animals by placing pseudo-gourmet names on the labels. Thus boiled pig snout becomes "Pork Stroganoff."

Steamed chicken nostrils become "Chicken Dinner."

Ground fish innards become "Seafood Surprise."

And then they put people on television to tell you that one brand of fish innards tastes better than another. How do they know? Either they have found a cat that can talk or some geek comes in once a week to taste cat food. If it *is* the latter, I wouldn't want to sit next to him on a bus before he had brushed his teeth.

If cat food manufacturers ever do take pity on cats and sell them real cat food instead of people food for cats, they can use the same euphemistic advertising to avoid nauseating cat owners. They won't bluntly say, "Canned Mouse Parts" or "Boiled Starling." They will say, "Petite Steaks" and "Mini-Squab."

But I guess a person can see some point in catering to what someone imagines to be a cat's favorite varieties of boiled animal parts. Cats can be picky.

(True, a few, small, neurotic dogs are also finicky. But they aren't really dogs in the complete sense. Somewhere back in the rat tunnels of time, they obviously bred with their prey and have become the nervous, crabby little twits you see today.)

Cats differ from dogs and from human teen-agers in that they eat slowly, tasting their food. And so, like adult humans, there are foods they will refuse.

There is no food a human teen-ager won't eat provided you incorporate it into a pizza.

That should give you some idea of how to dispose of any cat food that the cat can't choke down.

22. The People Marker

I'm a marked man.

Our cats mark me several times a day. They mark me as part of their territory. Call them fools but they post a sign before the world that they want to keep me.

They do that by rubbing against me with a gland that cats have above each eyebrow. You've probably noticed how a cat will kind of butt you gently, rubbing its forehead against you. What it is doing, to tell you the blunt truth, is rubbing its glands on you, smearing you with its marking potion.

But it is to us an imperceptible smear. It doesn't stain. It doesn't cause your hand to rot off if you pat a cat on the head. It's hormonal but it won't make weird people follow you home.

And let us count our blessings that dogs are not similarly inclined. It is enough that they mark trees the way they do without also laying an occasional stripe across the legs of their masters. Dogs would be a lot less popular if they did that. Anybody would be.

And if the truth be known, cats probably wouldn't be quite so popular if it were more generally known that they are in the habit of marking their owners. Indeed, my revealing that habit could put a dent in their popularity. But don't blame me. If they want to be popular, they shouldn't run around rubbing their glands on everybody.

Personally, I don't mind. It is certainly a more modest habit than running around indiscriminately smearing lipstick on people like some females I could mention. And it doesn't leave you with an odor detectable by humans, which is more than you can say for sitting next to a cigar smoker for a couple of hours.

Besides, who are humans to criticize the cat habit of marking things? A cat who is always staking out portions of the common world as his and his alone is little different from most world leaders.

Besides, it could be worse. A cat could rub one of his fish on you or even give you a couple of swipes with a little can of spray paint. But it is hardly insulting to have cats sauntering up to you several times a day and planting markers all over your calves and shins that read, in effect:

"Beloved companion of Sheldon."

"Dear friend of Delilah."

"Favorite feeder of Sterling."

Besides, turnabout is fair play. We sometimes put collars around their little necks, marking them as ours, making it possible to locate them when they are lost.

Similarly, the day may come when you wander away from the home. The day may come when you are adrift. But thanks to cats, nobody is ever so much alone that some possessive kitty isn't overjoyed to come rub up against him and declare to the world that this tattered old human is "Mine!"

23. Cat Dumping

I don't understand it. Human babies are a lot more trouble than cats but you rarely see a want-ad in the paper from someone offering to give away a human baby.

You see ads that read: "Moving. Must find good home for lovable tabby."

But you hardly ever see an ad that reads: "Moving to apartment building that won't permit children. Must find good home for adorable 12-year-old."

People just aren't in the habit of trying to unload a kid so they can move to some new city or apartment. For some odd reason, people tend to cling to children. They stay in the old apartment, or take the little nipper on to the next city with them, no matter what a loud, messy little pain in the neck he is.

But ads offering a dog or a cat are commonplace. And that is despite the fact cats are better behaved than children. It's amazing when you think about it. A cat never hits a baseball through the window. A cat doesn't hog the television set or spill its orange juice or leave the lid off the peanut butter jar. And when a cat doesn't get its way, it may grumble a little but it doesn't throw a tizzy and call you frog face.

It is only kids who do stuff like that. So you could understand it if a person tried to use a move to Montana as an excuse to dump a kid on someone else:

"Moving to Montana. Must give up housebroken three-year-old son. Good mouser."

People don't do that. People get attached to children for some remarkable reason.

On the other hand, people normally get attached to dogs and cats for equally remarkable reasons. But you could understand why a dog owner would get tired of a dog's uncivilized habits and try to pawn it off on the public in an untruthful classified ad that says the dog is housebroken and disciplined and quiet and all that other stuff that no dog is for any length of time. That's why they call them classified ads—because the real reason the advertiser is getting rid of the mutt is classified.

The real reason the family is dumping the dog isn't because they are moving to Montana; it's because they have come to their senses and pray God to be liberated from the damned thing. Dogs are even more trouble than kids.

I am similarly suspicious of ads offering to part with a pussycat. People don't ordinarily do that. People normally get so brainlessly attached to their cats that they insist upon taking them along, loose hair and all, wherever they go.

So why is the cat in the classified ad an exception to that rule?

I suspect something has gone sour in the relationship. I suspect a divorce in the making.

Things don't usually go that wrong with a dog. The kind of people who love dogs don't expect a full partnership. And some human marriages are the same. They thrive on a master-slave arrangement—the wife playing Mommy or the husband playing Big Daddy. That's pretty much what dog ownership is all about—a genuflecting fool groveling at the feet of the Adored One.

People tend to take up cat ownership for a different reason—because they prefer a more balanced relationship, an even-handed partnership rather than a dominant-subservient arrangement. The strong personality of most cats makes a balanced relationship feasible. Cats can hold their own in any contest for household supremacy.

If they could vote, cats would support equal rights for women and dogs would oppose it. I suspect that those few women who oppose equal rights for women are dog owners. They are comfortable with a servile kind of relationship and hope to conserve it.

But cats understand the specialization in household chores that takes place in a balanced marriage. For instance, in my marriage, it is I, the stronger one, who mows the lawn, and she, the cleaner one, who gets down on her hands and knees and scrubs the kitchen floor.

It is she, the seasoned, skilful one, who irons my socks and underwear. And it is I, the remarkably articulate one, who thinks up the words to use on the lawnmower when it won't start.

Similarly, it is my wife and I, the more affluent ones, who buy the cat food. And it is the cats, the tacky ones, who supply our home with all its bent sparrows and partially munched mice.

We supply the petting and they provide the purrs.

But I suspect there comes a time in some relationships when somebody stops carrying his share of the load and the whole thing falls apart. Somebody gets lazy and sloppy. Somebody forgets to pet. Somebody neglects to purr. Somebody grows complacent and sits around in a tiny T-shirt, sucking down little beers, watching cat food commercials on television and letting love die.

And then one day it is plain to everyone that pet and pet owner have lost the thread of their relationship, the ties that bound them together. Somewhere along the line, they grew apart and the time has come when the whole thing will work no longer. Something's gotta give. Somebody's gotta go.

And so an ad is placed:

"Must give away adorable, slightly worn butler. Great petter in the right home."

24. Sheldon The Ripper

The more vile the criminal, the more likely it is that his mother will insist he is innocent.

If somebody is arrested for 14 axe murders and a parking violation, you can almost bet that the guy's mother will show up at the courthouse insisting to every reporter who will listen that it's a bum rap, that the little dickens is blameless. Somebody must have knocked him unconscious and framed him by placing the weapon in his hands—14 times over the years.

You never see a case where somebody is arrested for 14 axe murders and a parking ticket and the press reports that his mother said he was always a little rat, that his birth wasn't the last time he was a pain in the rear and that she thinks he ought to fry.

Mothers of little rats are into denial. And in one sense, who can blame them? It must be hard enough for them to end up with a child like that without admitting—least of all to themselves—that he really did do all that.

And so they don't admit it. It's just too painful.

Besides, even the mother of an axe murderer loves her baby. Loving kids, no matter how weird they are, goes with the territory of being a mother. Nobody ever accused mothers of being open minded about their offspring.

Parents differ little in that respect from dog and cat owners. For instance, if you go to a neighbor and say, "I'm sorry to mention this but your dog keeps getting into my garbage" the neighbor will invariably cloud over and answer, "Well, you shouldn't leave your garbage out where it's so easy to get into."

Or he will look you in the eye, the soul of innocence, and say, "It wasn't my dog."

"Well, yes," you say, "I'm afraid it was. I looked out and saw a spotted yellow dog with three legs, one orange ear and a bright red collar climbing up on the garage roof where we try to keep the garbage out of his reach."

"Well," the dog owner says, "it must have been some other spotted yellow dog with three legs, one orange ear and a bright red collar because Poopsie would never do anything like that."

And when a dog runs out while you are jogging, knocks you to the ground and begins tasting your throat, the owner will always say the same thing, "Well, he never bit anyone before. You must have tantalized him."

And I did. I made the stupid mistake of growing a delicious throat.

Have you ever noticed that the only dogs who bite are those who have never bitten anyone before? If a dog bites somebody, the owner never says, "By George, that's the third time this week he's done that. I guess I'm going to have to do something about it. All these lawsuits are getting to be an inconvenience."

The owner says, "Well, he never bit anyone before. You must have kicked him or something."

Dogs are like guns. It is always the unloaded gun that accidentally goes off and hurts somebody. And it is always a dog that never bites that is allowed to roam free and bite somebody.

"It couldn't have been Poopsie who bit you. He wasn't even loaded."

People seem not to realize that a dog who never bites those who feed and love him is not the same thing as a dog that would never bite. He would never bite the members of his immediate family. Few of us would.

But he would bite the members of my immediate family, especially if he is dumb enough to think that a jogger running down the street where he lives is actually charging his house and preparing to threaten its occupants, the family that loves and feeds him. And of course, all dogs are dumb enough to think that. So there is no such thing as an unloaded dog.

All cats are also innocent in the eyes of their owners. All accusations lodged against my cats are wrong. Some bigoted, trouble-making neighbors may have suggested that our cats will occasionally dig in their flower beds but it's a lie. It's a cheap slander made up and spread by my enemies because they are so envious of our cats.

And our cats would never uproot those 14 small trees, as some have charged. It's a bum rap. The little sweethearts are blameless. They have all been carefully trained to dig only in their own yard. And all of our cats have been provided with little maps of the neighborhood to make certain they know their boundaries.

On the other hand, there are limits to such self-deception. And I am saddened to acknowledge that there may be some truth to the ugly speculation that one of our cats, young Sheldon, has been killing neighborhood birds and eating them raw. I am aware of frightened, angry talk in this part of town about our cat, the little guy we raised from a kitten. Behind our back they are calling him Sheldon the Ripper.

Nonetheless, the missus denies it, vehemently. It's a bum rap, she says. Not our little Sheldon, she says. Sure, she says, the little dickens is a tad mischievous, but her good little boy would never kill anyone. It must be that spotted yellow dog with three legs, one orange ear and a bright red collar who is killing all those poor birds. It certainly isn't Sheldon. She could never believe such a terrible thing about him.

I could. Every day or so, there is another bird missing from the neighborhood. And let's face it: Birds just don't vanish into thin air all by themselves. Somebody is knocking them off. Every day or so, you hear a little feathered scream and another bird is never to be seen again.

At least it will never be seen again outside our house. That's the problem. The bodies keep turning up inside our house. I see them all the time.

So does the missus.

"Strictly circumstantial," she says. "Nobody can prove a thing," she says. "Some jealous person who hates Sheldon is killing the birds and dragging their little bodies in here and trying to frame Sheldon. It's probably that spotted, yellow dog with three legs, one orange ear and the bright red collar. Sheldon wouldn't do that. Sheldon is a good boy."

"Sheldon," I remind her, "is the same good boy that you and I have both seen with a bird in his mouth coming in through the cat door."

"Circumstantial," she repeats. "A mere coincidence. He can't help it if some stupid bird flies into his mouth just as he is coming through the cat door. And he always takes the bird right back outside again the minute you yell at him. I'm sure he sets it free, calling after it to be more careful where it flies in the future. Sheldon is a good boy."

She'll never believe otherwise, of course. No mother ever will. Meanwhile, though, something must be done. And soon. Things are getting out of hand. The other day, I caught Sheldon dragging something a little larger than usual through the cat door.

It was the body of the spotted yellow dog.

25. Why Is A Cat So Rude When You're Getting Nude?

Have you noticed how a cat will stare at you while you're taking off your clothes?

Why is that? Are cats perverts?

The surface evidence suggests that they are. But I doubt it. The surface evidence is that, in our society, practically anyone who stares at you when you're naked is a pervert. Indeed, it's hard to think of anyone except my wife who could stare at me naked and not be considered a pervert, and I'm not so sure about her.

Nonetheless, there are people in our society, to whom we are not married, who can freely look at us when we are nude and escape being considered a pervert.

Doctors, for instance.

Nurses, for instance.

When you go to a hospital, people are coming in all day and lifting the sheet and examining your nakedness. Most of them are doctors and nurses.

In fact, doctors and nurses are almost as fascinated with our nakedness as our spouses, our cats and our perverts. You can hardly go into a doctor's office without some nurse showing you to a cold little room and telling you to shuck your shirt. Or the whole shooting match.

Except socks. If your feet are okay, they usually don't mind if you leave your socks on and I always do. You have to cling to whatever shreds of dignity this life allows and I may be standing there with my aging pectorals, my saggy paunch and practically everything else hanging out, but at least my feet are decent. At least my feet aren't nude.

But it still bothers me a bit to have some nurse I have never met tell me to go into this little cubicle and take off my clothes. It bothers me a lot if she works for an eye doctor.

I prefer private nakedness. But a cat butler has no privacy. About half the time when you're taking off your clothes, a cat will be staring at you with a curious look on its odd little mug. So it's possible that cats are perverts—and the worst kind, the kind who like to look at naked, saggy, aging men.

I feel especially uneasy when it is old Delilah peering at me, drooling as usual, giving me the creeps. I don't know if I look cute or just delicious

But what an opportunity we present cats if they are perverts. We give them the run of the house. We take no precautions. If your kids or your grandkids or your best friend from across the street are in the house and you need to change your clothes, you excuse yourself and go into the bedroom. You don't stand there in front of friends and family and change clothes.

But you can have a brand new cat on the premises, a cat you have just met, a cat who, for all you know, is on the official FBI list of certified perverts. And what do you do? You take your clothes off, right in front of a stranger. You get naked with a cat you barely know watching you take it off, take it all off.

But I doubt they are truly perverts, at least not most of them. For one thing, they not only look at you when you are taking off your clothes but when you are putting them on. It isn't nakedness that fascinates them; it's skinning yourself. It's taking your fur off and putting it back on again. It is putting on new fur of different shapes and colors. No other animal does that. So naturally, a cat is fascinated.

But that raises other questions: Do cats stare at us when we are dressing and undressing because they consider it strange? Are they laughing at us? If so, it wouldn't be the first person who ever laughed at me naked.

Or are cats jealous? Do they wish they could do that? Do they long to take off their heavy coats on a hot summer day? Do they wish they had a rain coat when the sky is letting go with a drenching shower?

Wouldn't they prefer to send their coats to the cleaners, the way we do, rather than licking the dirt off them?

Wouldn't anybody?

Or are cats simply perverts?

I don't think so, but I have my doubts about some of those nurses. Especially in the eye doctor's office.

26. Victory Over Toenails

Cats have conquered one of the principal heartaches of life—toenails. Cats have their toenails under control.

They are never socially embarrassed by forgetting to trim their toenails the way we are. That's because they don't have to trim their toenails. They just suck them up inside their feet.

I'm not sure how they do that but I wish I could do the same. I'm constantly forgetting to trim my toenails before some significant occasion. And I never realize I have forgotten until it is too late.

I rip the sheets lengthwise getting into bed in the guest room at a friend's house.

Or I realize I didn't trim the gnarly things when I climb into somebody's hot tub and notice that others in the tub are scooting over to the opposite side with a look of fear in their faces. Or I am strolling along a crowded beach and I accidentally puncture some kid's beach ball.

But most embarrassing of all was the time I was wheeled feet first into the operating room for a hernia operation and the last thing I remember is those twin stilettos, one at the end of each big toe, gleaming in the glow of the overhead lights. And I'm sure all those doctors and nurses noticed. I had forgotten to trim my nails again, as I do most years.

I don't know why. I guess it's because toenails are the farthest thing from my mind.

And the truth is, even if I knew how to suck them up inside my feet the way cats do, I would probably forget to do it. It's easier for cats to remember not to let their toenails hang out in public. They don't wear shoes. For them, the problem is always right out there in plain sight.

We have no such reminder. After all, you never really look at your toenails until it is too late. They are covered most of our waking hours. It isn't like fingernails, always right there, naked, in your face. In fact, it would be a lot easier to remember toenails if we were in the habit of eating with our feet.

Cats have the advantage. They sit around almost every day washing themselves, with first one hind foot and then the other right up in their faces where they can see the nails. They even wash between their toes with their tongues, for God's sake. So it's easy for them to talk. But if we were in the habit of using our tender tongues to lick among our sharp toenails, we would also notice our nails are too long or find a way to suck them up inside our feet.

Unfortunately, few of us are able to lick between our toes even when we have the urge to do so. Most of us have our hands full just bending over to trim our nails with a toenail clipper.

And the older we get, the harder that is. There are two reasons that is so. For one, our bodies become less flexible as aging gradually petrifies our parts. And worse, the more difficult it becomes to bend over and trim our nails, the more dense those nails become. The term for that is horny—as in horn. At least our nails become hornier as we age even if nothing else does.

That's probably part of the reason cats are so popular with older people. The more difficult it becomes to cope with our own nails, the more we admire the way cats can suck their nails up inside their feet when they see company coming.

But we need not be envious. After all, some of us older guys have learned to avoid haircuts by sucking our hair down inside our heads.

27. Do We Resemble Our Cats?

Some sages contend that we come to resemble our dogs and ours spouses after some years, which raises the question of whether we also resemble our cats.

Let us hope not. That would be overdoing it. It is unnerving enough to a man that he resembles a crabby cocker spaniel or that he comes to resemble the middle-aged woman he married. It would be the ultimate cruelty to learn that we also resemble some nasty, fat, defrocked tomcat.

But it is probably true that there are some similarities between us and our dogs and between us and our house-mates. We resemble our dogs and our mates for essentially the same reasons. It's partly a process of flattering ourselves. We tend to choose mates and dogs who resemble us to some degree from the start. For instance, we may fall for a woman because she reminds us of a favorite female relative physically or in her personality. In other words, she is the same mental and physical type as the members of our family. We like her because she is so much like us.

We choose dogs for similar reasons—not necessarily because they remind us of favorite female relatives but because they are the sort of dogs that favorite female relatives liked. And in truth, the dog's personality may remind us of Grandma or of Aunt Mildred.

And therefore of ourselves.

So we begin with a resemblance to our wives and to our dogs and then we intensify it by picking up habits and gestures from each other. If a wife or a dog is in the habit of scratching a lot or of whining during the evening news, we tend to adopt those mannerisms ourselves.

We also become alike by meeting each other halfway. Marriage, whether to a dog or to a woman, or even to a dog of a woman, is a series of compromises. If one spouse likes weak coffee and the other likes strong coffee, it isn't practical to brew two pots. So both husband and wife drink their coffee medium. Both give up coffee the way they really like it and drink it instead the way they both hate it. That's what marriage is all about—sticking together through adversity, including an adversity of your own creation.

And after a few years of fighting for use of the same stereo, she abandons Duke Ellington and he deserts Elvis and they both settle on Garth Brooks. In time, we tend to wag our tails at the same things that delight our wives and our dogs. In most cases, we begin somewhat alike and, eventually, grow together even more.

And a good thing, too. Better than growing apart.

That's why you see nervous people with nervous dogs and boring people with boring dogs, and even horny people with horny dogs—because puritanical people tend to refuse to have a horny dog around. They shoot a dog like that for its own good. And they would do the same for you if the law allowed.

But the point is that the dog and the dog owner didn't start out different and grow alike after spending some years together. People pick a dog because they identify with its nervous or boring or horny habits. They see themselves in the dog and they like what they see.

Thereafter the nervous dog makes the nervous person even more nervous and the boring man and dog are forever putting each other to sleep.

However, the terrifying part of all this is that we are likely to end up like our dogs and mates after living with them for years even if we begin the association with little in common. It's partly diet. Jack Sprat and his wife were actually a rarity. More frequently, we both eat the fat or the lean. We both tend to end up at about the same level of thin or plump because eating is one thing married people continue to do together for years after they don't do much else together.

And gravity tends to equalize all bodies. For instance, the older I grow and the more I sag, especially in the pectorals and other soft regions, the more I resemble my wife naked—an amazing development for both of us. The way things are going, it is only a matter of time before we end up with the same unisex appearance, she a balding woman with facial hair, and I a bearded man with the body of a wrinkled old woman.

And of course, many a person has grown old and sloppy right along with his dog. That would be burden enough to bear without also coming to resemble our cats. I don't think I want to end my life as a cranky old tomcat who doesn't do much but sleep, complain and eat.

But there is even worse:

Politics presents the most unsettling example of coming to resemble those we associate with. We tend to choose leaders who resemble us—leaders we perceive to be as selfish and as intolerant of others as we are. That may be harsh to hear but it is true. They are us. We look into these mirrors of mate and dog and cat and leader and the leader mirror presents the unkindest image of all.

By comparison with resembling our leaders, it's not so awful to resemble some old cat who sleeps and snores and spits up a bit but leaves us no worse than when we met and often gives us mirth and friendship by the hour. Cats are the opposite of leaders. The presidents and senators and governors we choose always look better in the beginning than they do after a few years. Cats are the reverse. They grow on a person. They don't let the job of being a cat go to their heads. They serve us well.

And the longer they rule our lives, the closer we grow to them. They have their quirks and their shortcomings but they are true and predictable and utterly honest, both in affection and in anger. You could say worse things about a person than that he resembles his cat.

28. Belling The Cat

There's one in every family—somebody who actually enjoys going out in the wild and exterminating his fellow animals.

In our human families, they are known as deer hunters and pheasant hunters and duck hunters and generals and presidents and prime ministers.

In our cat families, they are known as Sheldon.

At least in my cat family, the killers are known as Sheldon. He's the only one of our cats who regularly snuffs birds and mice.

It's just like people. Most people wouldn't kill another animal on a bet. They don't even stop to realize that the chicken and cows they chomp down are killed critters. They just sort of think of them as coming from the chicken breast factory and from the sirloin warehouse. When you go to a store, you don't think of killing. You think of porking out. And that involves meat, not cows. That involves chicken, not chickens.

It's kind of like war. There are times when, in the abstract, it sounds like a good idea, as long as nobody gets hurt.

Eating other creatures—and the unpleasant, unavoidable fact that they must first be executed —is simply one of those ugly aspects of life that a person tries not to dwell on. And if you dwell on it at all, it is to count your blessings that our role in this jungle points us toward eating killed cows rather than live ones. A live cow is an animal. A dead cow, by the time it gets to me, is nothing but a rump roast. Any killing that may have taken place—unbeknownst to me and without my specific prior approval—was by some cad I have never met and never want to meet.

The same is true of cat food. Surely that mushy brown stuff in the cans and that dry brown stuff in the packages was never anybody's mother. It's probably just flavored grain (and it's none of my business what it's flavored with).

Any cat of mine who eats that stuff wouldn't hurt a flea, even if you boiled the flea a little and dipped it in meat sauce (whatever that is).

All that self-delusion comes to a screeching halt the first time your cat brings home a wriggling dinner fresh from the cat's own, personally operated, fellow-creature slaughterhouse. All the fantasies of a peaceable kingdom come to a halt then and rude reality dawns.

If you have a cat who is a skilful hunter, then you are soon made to realize by the contents of its fangs that we are all at least de facto hunters (even the smug vegetarians if they use medicines and other products developed at the expense of animals and of defenseless plants).

When you see your cat with another living creature in its grasp, then you can no longer hide from the truth. You can no longer deny that cat food is birds and fish. You must admit that steaks are cows—with brown eyes.

And those armies we send off to distant wars are more than armies; they are men and women.

Consequently, we may come to know some remorse over what we are versus what we might want to be. But there is no blaming a cat for what it is and always will be, and that certainly isn't a vegetarian. The truth is that some cats are born to snooze and some are born to nibble on other critters. Some are sleepers; some are hunters.

Sheldon is our hunter whether we like it or not.

The other two cats are too dignified to do that any longer. They are like most of us—hypocrites who will not become killers themselves but hypocrites who are always eager accessories when it comes time to accept the proceeds of death from the cat food factories.

I state the case harshly to point out that we mustn't get too sanctimonious in judging Sheldon. On the other hand, I confess it is troubling to have a cat who goes out and kills something for breakfast each morning. It is like having a deer or a duck hunter in the family. And I do.

Actually, I don't mind so much the fact that some of my relatives go out in the wild and kill animals as much as I mind the embarrassing ritual that is part of their sport. The deer hunters in my family go outside in the winter and sleep on the ground. The duck hunters go outside in the chill of autumn and stand in cold water all day. The embarrassing part I mind is that both the deer hunters and the duck hunters in my family do that while saying repeatedly to each other, "Boy, oh, boy, isn't this fun!" There are days when I fear I may have to have them committed.

Sheldon behaves better than they do. He won't go outside in winter and sleep on the ground to get a mouse. He won't stand in cold water up to his privates to get a bird. He runs outside, snatches a bird or a mouse (or a small badger when he gets careless) and brings it straight into the house through the cat door.

Sheldon comes inside where it's warm. He lies down on the carpet or under the table or on the bed, meticulously dissecting his breakfast.

And while we may recognize that it is his nature to kill, we wish he wouldn't do it. At the very least, we wish he would do it elsewhere—perhaps in the house of some duck hunter who might appreciate his technique.

We wish Sheldon would join his owners and his cat colleagues in eating previously killed chicken and cat food and share with them the civilized fiction that no murders are involved in our respective dinners.

But it is not queasiness alone that prompts our dissatisfaction with Sheldon's habits. A cat butler grows weary of encountering little piles of this and that and coping with the remains. The fact is, Sheldon eats a good deal like King Henry VIII, gnawing off the flesh and then tossing the bones over his shoulder.

And the fur over his shoulder.

And the feathers.

The fact is, Sheldon is not merely a hyperactive carnivore but a slob as well.

On the one hand, it is amazing how much of a bird or a mouse a cat will devour. They don't leave much. Indeed, they leave a lot less than I would in their shoes. But there are always a few leftovers to be vacuumed, most especially including the mouse fur and the bird feathers. I can tolerate the fur and the feathers. It is the little leftover bird feet that force me to face the facts of life. It is the scrawny little feet that bring me face to face with what we really are, we cats and humans, we kindred carnivores.

On the other hand, let us not forget that birds are pretty quick to snuff a hapless beetle or a helpless worm if they get half a chance.

And let us not forget either that chicken simmered in garlic, olive oil and wine is well worth the alleged death of a chicken.

But then no one has to vacuum after my dinners, unlike the dinners of one cat I could mention.

It got to where I was spending half my time sucking up feathers and fur. And as he grew older, Sheldon started bringing a couple of critters a day home for dinner, whether they wanted to come or not. Something had to be done.

So we belled the cat.

The lady at the pet store sold us a little bell attached to a break-away collar—a collar that wouldn't snag on a limb and execute Sheldon while Sheldon was trying to execute birds.

The lady at the pet shop told us that she had belled her killer cat and it never brought home another body. The cat tinkled as it crept forward, warning birds and mice alike that trouble was coming.

So we strapped a bell around Sheldon's vicious little neck.

He brought another bird home that very night.

I'm not sure how he does it. I think he has learned to walk so softly that his clapper doesn't dangle.

Or maybe he hobbles slowly toward his prey on three legs, holding the bell with one front paw.

Most amazing of all, I thought I saw him the other day scattering bird seed and gently ringing his little Pavlovian bell each time the birds stopped by for a bite.

❖ ❖ ❖

29. Breaking Bread–And Mice

How appropriate it is that a large cat, hunkered down and content with the world, resembles a loaf of bread.

After all, man does not live by cat alone. And cat may not live by man alone. But each lives better with the other and the historic reason is bread.

Bread is what brought us together in the first place. Bread and mice. Cats started hanging around where we were thousands of years ago because the mice and rats used to hang around our grain. It was the rats and the mice in our grain that made cats feel welcome. Some people prefer a red carpet. A cat prefers a rat or a mouse. To a cat, a granary chock full of rats and mice is a welcome mat.

And the cats were truly welcome. In those days, you couldn't just pick up the phone and call an exterminator. When it came to saving the grain, cats were the only girls in town.

I suppose it didn't happen overnight. I suppose that when the first cat crept out of the jungle and tried to hang around the stored grain, people thought it was just another creature going after the grain. People probably threw rocks at the first cats to come around. They didn't know that cats wouldn't eat grain for several thousand years yet, and then only when it was flavored with meat juice and sold as bargain cat food.

And it probably didn't get the cat-human relationship off to a fast start that cats are inclined to use loose stuff like grain as an outhouse. But who could blame the cats if they looked at what humans proudly thought was the invention of the first granary and mistook it for the first litter box instead? It's all a matter of perspective.

Eventually somebody must have seen a cat catching a rat or a mouse and running off into the jungle with it. That must have raised some eyebrows because it is obvious that a creature that lives on rats and mice would be an asset to somebody with a lot of grain—especially if the cat could be persuaded to stop using the grain as a john.

Consequently, kitty litter was probably invented, as an alternative to loose grain, within days of the discovery that cats are as fond of rodents as humans are of bread. From that day forward, humans stopped throwing rocks at cats. From that day forward, humans embraced cats as useful.

And cats embraced humans as useful. We may have seen the cats as a means to maintain our stores of grain but they saw us and our grain as a means to maintain their source of rodents. Our food was a magnet for their food. So the cats decided to stick around.

From that mercenary beginning, the relationship has grown over the years to where we tolerate each other for broader reasons. And the transaction has changed quite a bit. Today, we give them canned food and they give us warm feet on a winter night. We give them shelter and strokes. They give us companionship and purrs. We give them a smelly litter box. They give us dead mice on the doorstep. Tit for tat.

But things just aren't the same any more. We buy our bread at the store, the same place they get their modern mouse substitutes. And thanks to pesticides and tight, modern granaries, we are no longer strictly dependent on cats for saving our food supply.

But they, on the other hand, would starve to death without us. Let's bear that in mind the next time one of the little twits is doing one of his snooty routines and expecting us to genuflect to his every whim. Cats need to bear in mind, all these many centuries later, that the shoe is suddenly on the other paw. For the first time in history, they need us a lot more than we need them. Except on hard days. On hard days, they serve a purpose. We don't need them so much any more to exterminate mice and run off the rats. But there are times when we need them to kill our loneliness and chase away the blues.

30. Cats And Immoral Women

I want it clearly understood that my attachment to cats is in no way a reflection on the morals of my mate.

There are those who would have you think so. The French, for instance. I am told that there is a French saying:

"A man who is partial to cats is a man who will marry an immoral woman."

Wouldn't you expect the French to be the ones to come up with something like that?

I am unclear as to the precise implication of the saying. Does it mean that a man who loves cats is irrevocably destined to marry an immoral woman whether he wants to or not?

Or does it mean that a man who likes cats is the sort of low-life who will marry an immoral woman if given half a chance?

I am also puzzled as to whether the saying is meant to imply that marrying an immoral woman is a blessing or a curse. Given the habits of the French, you cannot jump to the conclusion that they consider such a wife the worst thing that could happen to a man. I am a tad torn on that score myself and I'm not even French.

Indeed, "immoral" in the context of a French saying may not be intended as the slightest bit insulting. It may be intended to suggest, with approval, the direct opposite of egregiously moral, a condition not entirely conducive to a pleasant marriage. To a Frenchman, "immoral wife" may mean little more than "earthy." To a Frenchman, "immoral wife" may mean getting hitched to a good one.

But what is it about an attachment to cats and a preference for immoral women that the two inclinations go hand in glove?

Perhaps it is best to examine that question in the context of what we may infer from the other side of this coin:

"A man who is partial to dogs is a man who will marry a moral woman."

I suppose a dog and a moral woman are, on the surface, a heavy burden to wish on anyone. But there are men who would differ. There are men who would rather go out with their warm bird dogs and tramp around the wetlands in the autumn drizzle than spend a day inside with their cold wives.

But to me, that is probably one of the most appealing attributes of a cat: It doesn't expect you to go tramp around the wetlands in the autumn drizzle. It likes to stay inside where it's warm.

So do a lot of immoral women. Cats and immoral women, almost by definition, enjoy comfort and other pleasures.

Dogs and people who are intensely moral (in the French sense) are uncomfortable with being comfortable. Almost by definition, moral people don't trust pleasure. It just doesn't seem right to them. That's part of the reason moral people prefer dogs—penance on a leash. Intensely moral people believe that we are all sinners and owning a dog serves us right.

Cats and immoral women are a lot more laid back about that sort of thing. They aren't into guilt, though they generally have more reason to be than dogs and moral people.

So there is indeed some correlation between cats and immoral women. And we can be grateful for that.

But what does this say about my wife? After all, she is half French. And if I am partial to cats, then what does that say about her?

Only a dog would answer that question.

31. Spits Bath

If a person bathed the way a cat does—in public and by spitting all over himself—he would be swiftly arrested.

And rightly so.

I'll confess my intolerance on that score. I don't understand the way cats bathe, neither their manner of bathing nor least of all where they bathe.

By where they bathe, I don't mean that tired joke about washing their privates, though that's certainly as strange as it is gymnastic. When I speak about where they bathe, I mean in the living room.

And in the kitchen.

And in the dining room.

And even out on the patio, among assorted other astonishingly public locations.

The amazing thing about a cat is not what it washes. It washes everything, the same as you, though it would be a trifle more civilized to do that with a little wash cloth rather than with a tongue, if you ask me. But of course, no cat ever asks me or anyone else about such niceties. And, the truth is, what a cat washes is a personal matter and not really any of our business.

But where a cat chooses to park its furry little fanny while bathing is most certainly my business, especially when there is company present. The astonishing thing about a cat in that respect is that it bathes everywhere but the bathroom. The bathroom is the room provided for bathing and yet I have never seen a cat bathing in the bathing room. For instance, I have never seen Delilah with her little terry cloth robe on and a towel over one arm waddling down the hallway to the bathroom for her bath.

I have seen Delilah go into the bathroom for a drink from that rather uncouth bowl she routinely mistakes for a water dish, which is further evidence of how mixed up cats are in this matter. Delilah doesn't drink at the neighborhood tavern or even in the kitchen. She drinks in the bathroom, of all places.

But she doesn't bathe in the bathing room. She bathes in the cooking room, in the eating room, in the living room and even out on the patio in front of the neighbors without so much as a privacy screen or a pardon-my-immodesty.

Indeed, I doubt that cats care to bathe at all if there is nobody looking. All these years we have seen them washing repeatedly in front of us and in front of the whole world, ignorantly thinking that means they are clean animals, not realizing that all it means is that they are blatant exhibitionists. They bathe in front of us for the same reason they sit and stare at us while we dress—because they are perverts and they think we are the same.

But cats are wrong about us. We aren't like that. I bathe solely in the bathroom, in private and without spectators, no matter how much my trim trunk and supple paunch might indicate otherwise. You need not worry about me if you come to call. I will not sit around the living room or the kitchen or even the dining room, swabbing off this and that in front of company. And I don't know many people who would.

That is not because I am so puritanical. Indeed, I share with most of humankind the odd tendency to become less modest the older I get. I don't know why that is. But the more I sag and dangle, the more I jiggle and bounce, the more slack I acquire in my covering, the less I care who sees me a cappella.

That is the fascinating thing about aging. Our modesty is most intense when we look our best, when we are young. And the more we go to pork and pot, the less we care about who doesn't like the way we look. The older we get, the less things like that matter and the more it matters who is a hunk on the inside. The more we mature, the more our embarrassment falls away with our hair and the more careless we become about the way we prance around the house in our scanties, or worse.

But even an older person bathes in private.

In a bathroom.

With the door closed.

Unlike some cats I could mention. A cat washes in public. A cat likes nothing better than to saunter out in front of company, flop down on the carpet and start licking its body.

But that isn't the limit of their humiliating behavior. It isn't just that they wash in front of company. It's the way they wash:

They spit on their hands. And then they wipe their hands behind their ears.

You could understand it if a person who is in the habit of licking himself clean would not want to lick himself clean in some locations but would instead adopt the habit of using a little wash cloth to cleanse those parts. And of course, it is essential to devise some means of washing in locations where the tongue won't reach. After all, few of us can lick behind our own ears. And those who can find it painful.

But I confess I find it passing strange that a person who can't reach assorted locations with his tongue would skip the wash cloth and resort instead to spitting on his hands.

If that were a person and you called the police and said you had some guy at your house who was sitting in the middle of your living room washing his clothes—while wearing them—and was using his tongue to wash them, the police would find that interesting. And if you said the guy was at this very moment spitting on one of his hands and washing behind his ears with it, the police would rush right over.

If it were a person, we wouldn't put up with this indecency, this disrespect for our guests. After all, if cats won't use the bathing room to bathe, then we should at least train them to use the dishwasher.

I'll make a deal with the cats: If I stop embarrassing them by roaming around the house without my fur on, will they stop washing their clothes, ears and worse in front of my appalled visitors?

You scratch my ears and I'll scratch yours.

32. The Feline Gourmet

There is a reason why one cat will prefer to catch his own dinner while another cat will wolf down anything you shove in front of his face:

Some cats enjoy preparing meals for themselves. Some don't. They're just like us. Some of us like to be fed and some of us like to whip up a little gourmet treat.

There is no need for any of the cats at our house to prepare his own meals. Cat dinner, in the form of dry, scientifically-formulated and apparently-quite-tasty cat food, is constantly on the table, which is to say, on the floor. Cats aren't tall enough to sit at the table. They're far too short for that whether they are willing to admit it or not. So they squat down on the floor to eat, the way we do at a picnic. And that's what life is to a cat—one big picnic, albeit a picnic without Jello or potato salad. But I have never known a cat who wasn't desperately grateful that he didn't have to eat Jello or potato salad.

However, I have known a few cats who were anxious to overlook their rather sparse height, cats who were determined to get off the picnic floor and sit at the table, eating their dinner like anyone else in the family, cats who were unwilling to recognize that regular members of the family do not have bird breath or an unappetizing body-wide beard. I have known cats so blindly unrealistic as to expect that they might sit there barely peering over the edge of the table and nobody would ever notice they weren't human.

But we do notice. When my wife and I see some guy with hair on his forehead peering over the edge of the table, trying to look nonchalant, we spot it right away. My wife and I are quick about things like that.

Our cats are most inclined to try to eat with us when we have company. I guess they think we won't notice one more guest. But we do. And what a pathetic thing to attempt. A cat can't sit there at the dinner table with his eyes oddly glowing in the candle light and expect guests not to notice, not even in Idaho.

But most cats don't mind that the floor is their table. That's a lot easier for them. They are built close to the ground, which is where the floor is anyway so the floor is a pretty handy place for them to eat.

And most cats are content to eat cat food. Anything else is too much work for the average cat, just as anything but a TV dinner is more than some people want to bother with for their meals. (Personally I would rather eat cat food than a frozen TV dinner but to each his own.)

Cats are generally even lazier than people so they are the sort who almost unanimously prefer to have their food shoveled at them without any work on their part. But there are exceptions. Some cats enjoy whipping up something different on occasion—a fresh dinner of bird or mouse, for instance.

Similarly, some people find it relaxing after work to stop by the store, pick up a few raw ingredients and take them home to spend an hour or two transforming them into a gourmet treat.

Cats are quite similar to people in their individual peculiarities. Consider Sterling, for instance. Sterling doesn't care about gourmet food. Sterling cares about fuel. And the easier and faster it is the better. He is not only content to eat dry cat food night after night after night but he finds the most relaxed way to eat it—lying down with his face resting in the dish of food, just barely conscious, gradually grinding the chow in through his lunch hole.

It is a dinner and a posture not unlike that of the person who comes home and stretches out on the couch, watching rock videos while consuming a sardine sandwich and sucking down a cold, healing beer at the end of another madhouse day.

Sheldon is a different matter. Sheldon finds it fun to spend a little time preparing a meal. Sheldon relaxes after a hard day on the street by whipping up something special, usually his favorites, mouse or bird tartare.

That's why one cat will never go hunting but will be content to consume whatever slop you dump into its dish.

That's why another cat tires of that simple fare. That's why you occasionally find bird or mouse crumbs on the carpet. It's because some cats expect a little more out of life than dry cat food.

And they are willing to do something about it. They are willing, like any eager cook, to do the marketing. They are willing to go out in the bushes and bring home the ingredients, whether that be bird or that be mouse. Just as you and I might be willing to spend part of our evening recreationally chopping celery and mincing garlic if that produces a tasty result, so, too, is Sheldon ready to go visit his own little butcher shop. So, too, is he willing to spend part of his evening plucking his bird and mincing his mouse. After all, we get out of an evening no more than we put into it.

That is why some cats are constant hunters and others never stoop to such menial matters but simply keep their snorkels planted in their food dishes.

I suppose that's permissible in a free country. I suppose it is also a relaxing life to come home each night, take off your clothes and sit there in front of the telly munching a frozen supermarket pizza, never getting off the gastronomic floor.

And I suppose it is normal behavior to go sit in some trendy restaurant and let some smug waitress slop you and the rest of the lazy hogs. I am certainly not judgmental in these matters.

Nonetheless, you have to admit there is something rather admirable about a person who gets his nose out of the routine plastic dish and goes out in those bushes and catches his own celery, his own chicken breasts, his own fluffy little quiche.

There is something admirable about those who try to rise above their small culinary stature, reach for the gourmet moon and sit tall at the table in front of their own creations, their eyes glowing not so much from the candle's light as from the inner pride of having harvested and prepared their own tasty mouse.

33. Warning!

ATTENTION, ALL CATS!—It is strictly forbidden to bring outside food into the house through this cat door. Under no circumstances will you ever again bring in mice, birds, snakes, lizards or slow lawyers and eat them on these premises. Such foods are to be eaten outside only.

You will, of course, be permitted to enter the house and obtain a small glass of wine to be taken outside to eat with your mouse, bird, snake, lizard or slow lawyer. But the only food to be eaten inside the house is the prescribed daily ration of dry, clean cat food.

The cat butlers are unwilling to spend their valuable time vacuuming feathers, fur, scales or lawyer fluff. Until such time as you may learn to do your own vacuuming and have purchased your own Featherbuster or your own miniature Hair Hoover, please eat your wild dinners outside where they belong.

Any cat found to be in violation of this warning will be given a bath.

THE MANAGEMENT

34. The Combat Zone

I'll admit there is something invigorating about sitting in the waiting room of a veterinarian surrounded by barking dogs while your cat climbs your head. Nonetheless, the experience presents a question:

If veterinarians know so much about pets, why do they mix cats and dogs in the same waiting room?

Why do vets do that to us and to our cats? Why do they leave us in a situation where we must sit in a waiting room trying to keep our cat calm while some Saint Bernard is trying to have it for dinner? Indeed, one of the reasons cats end up in the waiting rooms of veterinarians is because dogs try to have them for dinner. Hence, there is something inconsistent about taking a dog-mangled cat to the vet and sitting there calmly waiting your turn while some other dog tries to mangle your cat.

You sit there calmly because the dog owner is sitting there in loose control of the dumb mutt that is going for your cat and so you feel some irrational urge to remain cordial and pretend like nothing is happening.

But of course, something is happening and neither you nor your cat care for it at all. Nonetheless, a dog owner will merely say, "No, Bruno!" once or twice, shooting you an ain't-he-a-cute-little-bow-wow smile as your horrified cat races around your person.

But you can't blame a dog owner. If a dog owner were smart enough to know a well-behaved animal from a crazy one, a dog owner wouldn't be a dog owner in the first place.

So I don't blame the dog owners. I blame the vets. They should know better than to construct uni-animal waiting rooms. Vets should try to put themselves in a cat's shoes. How would they like to go into a doctor's office with the flu and be chased around the room by a huge, slobbering virus?

But vets customarily seat small cats and large cat eaters side by side in the very same waiting room, without segregation or fang-proof vest.

Oh, I am told there are a few sensitive vets now who provide segregated seating for incompatible patients. But few do. Most veterinarians are like divorce lawyers, callously seating the warring parties together in the same waiting room while they await surgery. Most vets never have more than one waiting room despite the fact some of their customers are in the habit of eating some of their other customers.

On any given day, you will see in the same vet's office a pet mouse, seated next to a cat (a pet mouse eater) seated next to a dog (a cat eater) seated next to a horse (a dog stomper), seated next to a Frenchman (a horse eater). It's like asking Catholics and Baptists to attend the same church.

A cat owner is expected to sit there serenely in the waiting room while some brainless bowser keeps lunging at his cat and the cat climbs up on the highest thing he can find—his owner's head.

That is no way to cure a sick cat. Cats are no different from people in that respect. They are cured, not just by medicine, but by tenderness, by calm surroundings, by a good rest. It is not easy to achieve any of that if you are placed in the same small room with someone who is trying to kill you.

There is nothing comparable in human medicine, with the possible exception of those rare occasions when you end up seated in the waiting room next to the doctor's bill collector.

I have spent my share of time in a vet's waiting room with a cat climbing my head and with a dog trying to climb my body. Fortunately, I have sustained no injuries over the years, except to my wallet. In fact, I am one of those people you have heard about who owns $500 cats. That's how much we have invested so far in removing testicles, giving shots, stuffing the critters full of worm medicine and treating the standard 14 abscesses a year.

But better the extravagance than the alternative. The ghastly alternative in a former time was a few cents for a rifle cartridge. In an earlier era, when the only expensive animal treatment was reserved for something essential like a horse or a cow, cats that were feeling poorly were a luxury. In a prior time, the blunt fact is that the cure for any serious cat troubles was to send Kitty to that Big Catnip Field in the Sky.

But this is a more gentle era today. Today, we don't write them off. Today, we rush them to the vet the minute they turn up with some trifling ailment. And that is why so many of us own $500 cats. We pay for it on the installment plan, one abscess at a time.

But there is the unfortunate trade-off that it is not always a kindness to keep a pet alive. I sometimes wonder in that respect about Sheldon. He does not come from sturdy stock. He was born with that hole in his side that the vet stitched up. And he was born with arthritis as well. He has been in periodic pain on cold mornings since he was a kitten. I wonder if I do him a favor with these repeated visits to the vet. Perhaps the bullet of yesteryear was not always hasty.

And so I sometimes hesitate to take him to the vet one more time. Sheldon has had more than his share of rough days. And then, to pour salt in his congenital wounds, he must sit in the madhouse with all those dogs, waiting to be poked one more time.

But he is not alone. I see all those other cats in all those other laps, waiting their turns, mostly with abscesses—a condition, like a toothache, that does not go well with yapping dogs. I sit there among the cats and I see the pain—and the hatred of dogs—in their eyes.

What galls a person is to wonder how many of those abscesses they get from fights with dogs in the vet's office.

35. The Cat Drug Of Choice

A cat likes a little nip now and then. That's why they call it catnip.

Unlike humans, cats do not fall into categories of users and teetotalers. All cats nip at least a little bit. But some humans drink not at all. That leads other humans to the plausible but false conclusion that they must take up the slack. So they not only do their own drinking but also ingest the quota of drink assigned to those who choose not to imbibe.

Similarly, there is no law that all cats must dote on catnip, the cat drug of choice. And some cats like it more than others. But every cat will give it a sniff now and then.

And some cats, like those humans who believe they have to fulfill the quota of teetotalers, do more than their share. But no cat, no matter how square, will ever tell you that it is a sin to sniff catnip. A cat will never look down his nose at you if you want to sniff catnip when he doesn't. A cat might be largely indifferent to sniffing catnip most of the time but he will never resort to sanctimonious superiority, the teetotaler's drug of choice.

Cats do their nipping in a far different way than humans do theirs. Humans use their favorite drug, alcohol, in liquids. They drink it. That's why the habit is called drinking.

Cats roll on their favorite drug, catnip. And I suppose they call it rolling.

"Whata ya say, Lester, ya wanta go over to the catnip bar for a couple a rolls after work?"

And it is better that people drink their drug and that cats roll on theirs. It would be too messy for people to start rolling on their drinks, though they could probably roll on an unlimited number of drinks without getting arrested for drunken driving. However, people who go into a bar and roll on their drinks are a strong bet to get arrested anyway.

Cats aren't the only ones who roll on their favorite drug. Dogs like to roll on horse manure and on dead skunks. Manure and skunks are the dog drugs of choice. There is nothing a dog enjoys more than rolling on horse manure and skunks, with the possible exception of rolling on your new couch immediately afterward.

Rolling on manure and skunks is probably one of the most vulgar drug habits of all time, and even more likely to get you arrested than rolling on drinks, especially if you aren't a dog.

Some cat literature suggests that a cat's interest in catnip is sexual. And we're talking about some pretty kinky stuff here because they don't mean that catnip is an aphrodisiac in the ordinary sense. They don't mean that a cat gets high on catnip and then gets frisky and heads for some nearby singles alley looking for action.

They mean that a cat gets horny over the catnip itself, that the cat takes a few hits off his weed and then starts rolling all over it like it was some beloved and eager tabby.

I don't mean to judge but frankly, that strikes me as a little sick. What if some guy walked into a bar, had a couple of glasses of chardonnay, lost control of his inhibitions and started necking with his glass. Talk about stunts likely to get you arrested.

I suppose there are people who love their wine more than they could love another person. But that doesn't make it normal or right to fall in love with your aphrodisiac.

However, who are we, with our little two-by-four minds, to expect that we might comprehend these mysteries of the cat world? Who are we to assume that we are morally superior to our cat friends just because they roll on pungent weeds and we don't?

Besides, I am too busy preparing dinner to judge others. I have invited the neighbors by this evening to roll on some fried chicken and zinfandel.

36. She Ran Out Of Stuff Before Finishing Him

With hindsight, we realized that Sheldon's mother ran out of stuff before she was through making him. And he was from a recklessly inbred line.

He paid with his life last week for those mistakes of people. And his creation was an error that my wife and I will never be an accessory to again. Why should a cat suffer just so we can feel softer fur?

Sheldon was a Balinese. In defense of us, we didn't know when we got him what he was made of. All we knew was that he was an uncommonly handsome variation on Siamese cats with fur as soft as the down on a duckling's belly. That was enough. We saw such a cat in another home. And of course, we wanted one.

But that is no way to buy an animal. You shouldn't start ordering them by design like new automobiles. You shouldn't ask them to remodel the fenders. You should take cats like kids—the way they are, the way they have always been, the way they have been popping out of the factory since they and the Egyptians first brought our kind together.

You shouldn't order animals with white sidewalls. You shouldn't specify soft seat covers. You shouldn't order blue headlights. You shouldn't offer to pay more for mere appearance.

When you do that, you tempt breeders even more reckless than you are to focus too tightly on characteristics less significant than personality. You encourage them financially to turn breeds inward upon themselves, intensifying a color, encouraging a shape and neglecting health in the process.

The so-called Balinese are the result of two separate mutations about 40 years ago. The last I heard, that was all the mutations of that type there had been. So Sheldon's genes came entirely from the narrow base of those two families—like two neighboring hillbilly families inbreeding the health out of each other.

Worse, the mother cat who gave birth to Sheldon had been turned into a kitten factory, a machine-gun mom, spewing litters by the dozens. I think she ran low on cat stuff by the time she got to him. We discovered not long after we got him that he had been born with that hole in his side.

And then came the arthritis. It turns out he was born with flawed bones, with some terrible congenital condition in his hips and backbone. From the time he was 2 years old, he was like a little old man on cold, rainy days, crippling around the house in pain. But it was only periodic. He looked so healthy that we thought at first he was respraining a leg. So we delayed.

The odd part is that, on his many good days, he was our most active cat. And unlike some inbred animals and people, it didn't seem to affect his brain. He was, if anything, our brightest cat, and certainly the most dependent on human company. As my wife would lie in bed reading,

Sheldon would cuddle up beside her and fall asleep with one paw hugging her arm.

But there were soon too many days when he was off in a corner, listless and tattered, his blue eyes clouded with pain. He was getting worse before our eyes. Fortunately, the laws of the state of Idaho are more humane when it comes to deciding such matters for animals than for people. And so Sheldon now chases mice somewhere over the rainbow, free from pain, as the preachers always say.

He was only five. And he leaves two wiser friends behind. We won't do that again. But it makes a person wonder when, in this appearance-crazy country, we will stop trying to change people and animals. Will the day ever come when we take them the way they are, blue headlights or brown, soft fur or coarse, short or tall? What's wrong with a cat who looks and acts and feels like a cat? And what does it matter what kind of fur he has if he merely does what cats do best—if he lies down next to you and hugs your arm while you read a book? How can you improve on that?

37. Don't Tread On Me

A person wouldn't lie down and nap on an elephant path. Why do cats lie down in the places where the elephants they live with are most likely to walk?

If I lived in a jungle, my favorite places to stretch out would be the places where the elephants never walked. It is no picnic to be walked on by an elephant.

Or by a human, if you are a cat. And cats frequently get stepped on. But they learn nothing from it. They cry out and curse you and go sulk in the corner for a bit. And then they go right back and lie down on the elephant path.

Why aren't cats more cautious of the big elephant feet they live with? Why do cats lie down in the middle of the kitchen, in the hallway and on the stairs? Why do cats avoid places where we are unlikely to step? Why do they prefer those exact locations where our feet are most likely to strike? Do cats have a foot fetish or something? Are cats the kind of sick people who relish getting stepped on by the ones they love?

Or is this some kind of insurance scam where they let you step on them, scream whiplash and then sue you for every can of cat food you own?

Maybe cats, noticing that they have fibers all over their bodies, think they are rugs. Cats certainly look like rugs, though they are much too thick to walk on comfortably. And they are much too noisy to be a rug. It's disconcerting to walk on a rug that screeches. So if that is their game, cats should give it up. They make lousy rugs.

But cats, if they stay out from under their elephants and live, make great pets. And that's fair. Rugs make lousy pets but rugs make great things to walk on and we should all stick to what we do best.

Cats have to learn that they make better pets without footprints on their faces. But I suppose it's one of those things like seat belts. Practically everybody knows you are safer with a seat belt in an accident than without one. But there are still a lot of people who won't wear seat belts because they don't think they will ever be in an accident.

Maybe cats know that it is dangerous to nap where elephants walk. Maybe they even acknowledge that a lot of cats get footprints all over them that way. But it'll never happen to them. It always happens to the other cat.

There are also those drivers who have been thrown head first into the windshield too many times. They will tell you that, technically, you're safer without wearing a seat belt than with one. They believe that you're better off to be "thrown clear," as it is known in the folklore of the road. Oddly enough, they believe it is better to end up outside the car with the car rolling over the top of you than inside the car with the car rolling over the top of somebody else that you don't like nearly so well.

Similarly, there may be those cats with a few bricks short who believe that it is safer to lie down on the floor right in front of the sink where the humans usually stand. Maybe they believe it is better to be where you will be accidentally kicked over into a safe corner—"kicked clear," as it is known in catlore—than to nap in the corner where you won't be braced for it if some careless human does start walking on your face.

Or maybe cats endure the modest pain of letting us walk on them for malicious reasons. This could all be some cruel cat sport. They could be faking the shrieks because we hardly ever come down on them full force, though they scream their lungs out if you so much as touch them. They may be working us, deliberately positioning themselves where they will be touched by a toe, bellowing bloody murder, accepting the pats and tidbits we give them as apologies and then going off with the other cats somewhere to laugh their hairy heads off. They may be making fools of us.

If you think your cat is making a fool of you, why not take him out in the jungle and tie him down on an elephant path.

We'll see who has the last shriek.

38. A Fuzzy Old Friend With A Bullet In Him

You would think when an old friend has been shot that he might mention it to you.

But he never did.

Sterling has been my friend and footwarmer these many years. He sleeps on my feet when I am stretched out on the couch watching football. Sometimes I sit on that same couch with my laptop computer in my lap (yes, that's why they call them laptop computers. Computers you rest on your head are called headtop computers, though I don't believe they are selling well.)

As soon as Sterling hears the keys clicking on the computer he strolls in and curls up by my feet. He just seems to sleep better with me around. And in truth, I feel the same way. It's easier to take a couch nap with a cat on your feet. (But it can be difficult to take a cat nap with a couch on your feet.)

Sterling also helps me with the dishes. When I sit there watching football and eating cereal, he cleans the remaining milk from the bowl for me afterwards. (Yes, of course, I put it in the hot, sterilizing dishwasher. I like cats on my feet but not cat spit on my cereal.)

It is a compliment to our pets that, knowing we must one day pay the pain of losing them, we take up with them nonetheless. We like them so much that we accept the fact we must one day live with a hole in our heart.

Women generally outlive men and so a lot of wives pay the same compliment to their husbands.

Sterling is lucky. He will probably have me as a friend for the rest of his life never knowing an empty day without me.

But it's just a matter of time before I get cold feet, before my foot warmer is gone.

I've been braced for that loss for some time because Sterling nearly died four years ago. I have been given to understand that the affliction may shorten his life. And he's already nine.

I realized one day four years ago that I hadn't seen him for a day or so. I searched the house and finally found him in a corner of the basement, barely able to sit up. He was sick as a dog.

It was some sort of big-time infection but a tenacious vet pulled him through. However, the vet warned that such ailments often return. He said Sterling might live to a ripe old age. Or he might last six months.

And so every time Sterling gets ill, I wonder if this is it—the way wives married to aging husbands must. That's what I did this past week when Sterling started sneezing as we watched football together. He had some kind of a cold. But there seemed to be more. So the vet, puzzled at his condition, X-rayed him and discovered something astonishing:

Sterling had been shot!

Apparently it happened four years ago at that time he was so ill. He still has the pellet healed up inside him.

I guess the wound was infected or something at the time and that was the source of his earlier sickness.

I have no idea who shot him or what the motive was— some rotten kid doing some city hunting, some cranky old bird lover who mistook him for a killer, maybe another cat with a grudge.

But a thing like that shakes a person, knowing that some stranger out there with some ugly impulse actually shot one of the dearest friends you've ever known.

And in a strange way, I feel guilty. When a friend of yours has been shot and he's lying there on your feet every night, it seems you should notice.

Maybe we should turn off the football games and talk more.

39. The Cat Toadies

Most presidents forget how to drive by the time they leave the White House.

And some emerge from all those years of having everything done for them unable to dial a long-distance telephone call. In fact, that may be how we have avoided World War III for so long. Presidents are so pampered that they have forgotten how to push a button.

The wonder is that they don't forget how to walk. They can go all the way to Europe without walking more than a couple of steps. They take an elevator from the White House living quarters. They board a helicopter on the White House lawn. The chopper takes them to the airport where they don't have to stand in line with the peasants but are deposited at the foot of the airplane stairs.

Oh, sure, they do walk a few steps now and then. But they don't have to. And in the future presidents won't even do that. There are always more than enough big, strong toadies in the White House who would pick up the president and carry him to a car or an elevator whenever he says the word.

And that seems right. After all, a queen bee doesn't walk. A queen bee's loyal toadies see to it that she doesn't have to. And Lord knows, a president has enough to do without walking. Besides, somebody that important shouldn't have to walk.

To a cat, you can't get much more important than you are when you find a couple of cat toadies to feed and worship you. That's why some cats hardly ever walk. That's why cats lie around all the time, waiting for us to lift them from the bed and place them on the floor with their faces in the cat dish, just like a president.

They say we have no royalty in this land. But it isn't so. We have cats.

And with each passing year, we treat our presidents more and more like royalty—and like cats.

Can a nation long endure if it fawns over its presidents the way it fawns over its cats?

40. The Breakfast Stomp

Cats are supposed to be night people but they sure behave like day people.

Day people dote on getting up at some ungodly hour. Worse, they believe that all decent people should do the same. And they make it their job to see that everybody else becomes decent.

Cats, for a different reason, are also determined that everyone get up when they do. Cats make no moral judgment in the matter. But they do make a breakfast judgment. They believe that once they are ready for breakfast it is indecent of you to remain in bed.

Human day people are more moralistic in the matter. They look down on those who enjoy sleeping in. Looking down on others is a way of ratifying their fetish about rising early.

Night people aren't that way. You never hear of a person who sleeps until noon lording it over an early riser. Night people have too much pride to stoop to common superiority. It is only day people who stand atop Mount Righteousness looking down their noses at weaklings who tarry in their beds.

I don't know whether we night people are essentially immoral or not. I do know that morning is not a time when we function well. The trouble with morning is that it happens at such an early time of day. I think our blood is slower then or something. I know our mouths don't work right in the morning. It's hard for us to think and talk at that time of day.

Not so day people. My wife is a day person and she hits the floor with her motor running. She's chipper and chatty and ready for conversation. All day people are. And they don't understand that just because a night person is finally up in the morning and courageously standing on his feet doesn't mean that his mind is warmed up and working yet. Day people want to rush you into conversation. The minute I crawl out of bed, my wife asks me things like, "What do you think will be the three most significant aspects of our relationship with Iran 20 years from now?"

I am standing there, 10 seconds out of a sound sleep, having trouble remembering what year it is, and she is grilling me with complex questions requiring more than a no-grunt or a yes-grunt. I am struggling with a cold mind just unhooked from a pillow and she wants a treatise on Iran.

Day people live in only two gears—wide awake and asleep. They don't know that night people live in three gears—wide awake, asleep, and a few hours each morning of regaining consciousness.

Day people are like birds. Birds won't shut up in the morning and let a person sleep. Birds are day people— loud, talkative day people. And that's probably why house cats, contrary to popular opinion, are also day people. Each morning when the birds start jabbering, a cat hears it as the sound of breakfast and is suddenly wide awake. (Actually, one of our cats, Delilah, is neither a day person nor a night person. She sleeps day and night, rousing briefly for meals. Delilah is a food person.)

It is no mystery why day people have become the saintly ones in our society while night people are the sinful ones. It is a throwback to our agrarian past when we were all farmers and there really was some need to get up and get moving when the sun did. If you didn't make hay while the sun was shining, your family could starve to death. And people back then were pretty stuffy about a guy who let his family starve to death. They looked down on guys who let their families starve.

It was during that time that people came to believe that those who overslept were immoral. And now, even though most of us work inside under electric lights, the baseless notion persists that we who sleep a little later are morally unclean. But we cling rather selectively to these beliefs from our farming past. During that period, there was also an economic reason for farmers to have 10 or 12 kids if they could manage it. Kids were the first farm machinery and you couldn't make it without them.

Or without getting up early.

You will notice the inconsistency of the day people in our own time. They are still caught up in the farmer belief that it is moral to rise early but they have conveniently forgotten about producing 10 or 12 kids. And one makes about as much sense as the other these days.

But that doesn't stop day people from trying to cure you of your wicked ways. Oh, they won't often come right out and holler you awake, telling you all decent people should be up by now and that they are going to make you decent if it kills you. No, they are never so direct.

They stomp around the house, slamming doors, moving chairs across the floor, absentmindedly humming "The

Battle Hymn of the Republic," throwing open a window so you can hear the damned birds chirp.

Cats are also stompers but they are more forthright about it. When they are up and ready to be fed, they want you up, too, and they go right to work on getting you out of the sack. They do not stomp around the house. They stomp around the bed with you in it.

They have discovered that humans, whether day people or night people, tend to rise earlier when stomped on than when not stomped on.

And cats don't hum "The Battle Hymn of the Republic." They bellow. They bitch. They moan.

And of course, they get their way. What my moralistic mate can't accomplish, a cat, crabby with hunger, can.

But it could be worse. I'd rather be roused by the cat stomping on me in its furry feet than by the wicked wedgies of my mate.

41. The Naked Brows Of Grief

The evidence all pointed to one conclusion:

I was going to have to shave off my eyebrows. The cat was missing.

There was a period in ancient Egypt—the only other culture to go as gooney over cats as we have—when the members of a family whose cat had died would shave the hair off their eyebrows. It was a sign of mourning.

It was also a sign of somebody with cold eyebrows.

I do not know the derivation of the custom. But you could do worse. There have been cultures in history, including ancient Egypt, when a death in the family meant several other members of the family would also be buying the farm, or the pyramid, or whatever it was they bought in those days when they bit the dust. If the head guy died, they would snuff a lot of others to keep him company in the tomb, including not only the missus but also the cat.

The ancient Egyptians can be grateful that the custom wasn't a two-way street, that the death of a cat didn't prompt the religious authorities of the day to bump off the entire family to keep Kitty company in the Hereafter. Indeed, cats were so numerous in that land then, and so short-lived, that if the custom had been to put whole families to sleep upon the death of their cats, there would soon have been no Egyptians.

But there was a period during cat-crazy ancient Egypt when families did sacrifice a part of themselves upon the death of their kitty. If a cat died, all the members of the cat's human family would assassinate their own eyebrows.

It was their version of wearing black. It was their way of saying, "You think you've got it rough; look at us. Our cat died. And so did our eyebrows—in memory of Fluffy"

Don't ask me why they chose to remember their little loved one with bald eyebrows. I know it isn't strictly appropriate. The appropriate remembrance upon the death of a cat would be to glue hair all over your face and try to be one in appearance with the dearly departed.

But it is only the form I question, not the sentiment. For their own bizarre Egyptian reasons, they saw naked eyebrows as the ultimate expression of their grief and that should be good enough for anyone. Sure, it's a little weird but it is traditional in the history of cat worship.

However, for that reason, I was a tad concerned when my wife pointed out that Sterling had been missing for 24 hours. I had just been reading about the Egyptians and their odd eyebrow habit. And I confess my first thought was not for Sterling. My first thought was, there go the old eyebrows.

I guess I'm a little stuffy but I am uneasy with the thought of being a conservatively-dressed, straight American male and going out in public in my little blue suit and tie with bald eyebrows.

But it could be worse. The custom could be more appropriate and then I would be uneasy about going out in public with hair glued all over my face.

However, there was a better than average chance that Sterling hadn't bought the pyramid. My wife tends to panic a bit. If she hasn't seen a cat for a couple of hours, she starts fretting over the probable demise of a hairy loved one. She also has the odd habit, when we are miles away on vacation, of looking wistfully off into the sunset and saying, "I wonder if any of the cats are dead."

You have to understand that my wife is a mother. She worries about stuff like that. I have tried to break her of the habit. I have explained to her that we have enough real tragedies to worry about in this life—war, disease, famine, hot polyester slacks—without worrying about cat deaths that haven't happened. My wife is always killing cats like that. And they are always resurrected when we get home and the groundless worry over the cats gives way to the fact of their fawning presence.

However, this was a little different. Sterling had vanished for 24 hours. That wasn't normal. He's a wimp and a Papa's boy. He can't go 10 minutes without a bite to eat and a cuddle.

And yet he was not to be found.

I am not a cat killer like my wife. I am an optimist. I'm more inclined to look wistfully off into the sunset and say, "I'll bet Lincoln isn't really dead." And so, presented with the fact Sterling was overdue, I considered all the sunny alternatives:

He had been captured by a lonely little girl whose mother would explain to her that the kitty obviously had another home. They would liberate Sterling first thing in the morning.

Or he was off on a catnip bender with a few close friends and had lost track of the time.

Or he had been savagely attacked by a gang of mice but had fought them off, breaking his leg in the process, and was even now just a few minutes away, bravely dragging himself home.

On the other hand, it had been a long time. And the price of having a cat door is to run some risk of losing the cat. Cats are like children in that respect. You can chain them to the bed and keep them safe from the outside world—and make them weird in the process. You can protect them— and deny them the chance to soar.

Or you can install a kid door in their life and let them go when they feel like it. But that's the trouble with a kid door. It has sharp edges. It cuts the apron strings.

Similarly, a cat is happier if you install a cat door in its life and let it roam free, as is its nature.

However, you do that with the knowledge that there may come a day when your cat becomes a little flat hairy thing beneath the wheels of a truck.

But better than chaining the cat to his bed.

Sterling loved to roam free, and now he was missing. Maybe he had bought it somewhere out there.

Of course, it was all the fault of my wife, to hear her tell it:

"It's that collar I bought him," she said. "He's hung himself climbing a tree."

Why do we do that? What is it about the death of somebody we love that sends us searching for ways to blame ourselves? There's hardly a freshly widowed spouse who hasn't said, "I wasn't as nice to Harry as I could have been. Maybe he wouldn't have lost the will to live if I had stopped punching him in the mouth."

Or, "I wish I hadn't given Eloise that will-writing kit and that gun."

Or, more commonly, "I was so cranky the last time I saw Chester. I wish I had been kinder to him. I wish I had told him how much I loved him."

It's guilt. But it isn't just guilt that we weren't loving enough to the departed kitty or spouse. It's also guilt that we are still alive and they aren't.

And so we want to punish ourselves. We want to wear sack cloth and ashes. We want to flog ourselves.

We want to shave off our eyebrows.

We want public humiliation because we made it and the cat croaked. And I'll admit, there are few ways better to humiliate yourself than walking around with bald eyebrows, with your guilt stripped naked before the world.

And sure, the day Sterling disappeared, I bought into that a little. I was thinking that, well, yes, I probably could have bent over and patted him on the head a little more often.

But then we remembered the garden shed. I had fetched a shovel from the garden shed only the day before. We opened the door and there he was, thirsty, hungry and swearing at us like the cranky little bastard he is. What an ingrate.

However, I did bend over and give him a little pat on the head. I guess I probably should give him a little more attention in the future, too.

And the fact is, we probably should also bend over more often and give our spouses a little pat. You never know when you might lose your eyebrows.

42. The Old Kitten Escapes To Chase Her Tail

I heard a frantic noise one recent morning that sounded like two animals chasing each other.

I turned to see one animal chasing itself.

Delilah, like many of my older friends, still chases her tail in the sunlight, spinning in a tight circle as the tip of her tail manages to stay half a step ahead of its pursuer. People and cats get old gradually, not all at once. And hardly anybody gets totally old. There is a kitten in all of us that escapes once in a while and frolics in the sun.

More in spring than at any other time. We are all a little younger in the spring. And so our old cat was chasing her tail. She was spotlighted by a spring sunbeam and behaving like a kitten. A person can understand that. We all feel the urge to play this time of year. I feel like chasing my own tail these mornings as the sun comes back inside the house after being away all winter.

So that was not unusual conduct for a cat. Nonetheless, you expect an old cat to be more dignified. She is 14, which is the equivalent of about 60 or so for a human and the equivalent of about 900 for a cat who crosses the street as often as she does. But the truth is, her kittenish conduct is also the equal of the way older humans behave. They almost all retain some spark of youth throughout their lives. After all, life is a journey, not a series of doors firmly marking the line between one kind of conduct and another. People get dignified gradually, not all at once.

And like Delilah, they never quite get all the way dignified. They chase their tails less frequently as they get older but there are days when the kitten wells up in all of us if we're lucky.

When you are a kid, you expect to grow up. You expect a day will come when you are no longer a kid. You expect to become an adult by the time you are 19 or 20 or 21. And you do.

And you don't. When you say someone is 20 years old, that is merely an average. One moment he's 12 and the next he's 40. People can be awfully silly and awfully serious at that age.

And at 40.

And at 80.

The 80-year-old is old more often than he is young. The older you get, the more old moments you have and the more involuntary dignity. The older you get, the fewer moments you have when the giddy kid jumps out. But few 80-year-olds are totally old. The kid is always there, just behind the eyes.

And few 2-year-olds are never old. Children behave like children most of the time, but there are moments when they become old and grumpy.

In fact, anyone who has been in the vicinity of a volatile 2-year-old knows that there is no crabby old man as hard to get along with as a toddler on a bad morning. Indeed, one could make a case for the premise that a 2-year-old is older than an 8-year-old and sometimes older than an 80-year-old.

And they are worse in winter. We are all a little older in winter.

So we don't begin our lives totally young and then finally grow up one day. You never finish growing up if you do it right. The unhappiest people on earth are those who grew all the way up.

We begin our lives mostly young with grumpy times now and then and end our lives mostly old with silly time-outs from that somber assignment of acting our age.

Best of all, when Delilah chases her tail like a kitten, she becomes a kitten again. It takes her to a time when she was small and quick and chased her tail all day long in the warm spring sun of yesteryear.

That's what you see in those pictures of old cats sitting in old laps in nursing homes. An otherwise bored and grim person will light up with a cat in her lap.

And the cat lights up, too. As the gnarled hand pets the graying fur, they both purr. They are a child and a kitten again. And the old child laughs as the aged kitten chases her silly tail in the springtime sun.

43. A Powdered Bird Diet To Make Fat Cats Slim

I feel I have failed as a parent and as an American.

I have just purchased diet food for my cats. That is a sad commentary on something. And it is no compliment to me or to this society or, least of all, to the hairy lard buckets at our house.

Talk about an affluent society. Talk about fat cats literally. A society that has to develop diet food for pets is the pinnacle of self-indulgence.

And speaking of self-indulgence, in fairness to me, this is more the cats' fault than it is mine. After all, I didn't hold a gun on them and make them stuff their faces full of food. They did it all themselves. As a result, Delilah looks like an upholstered football with legs.

And since Sterling is a Siamese he has always been the color of a seal. Now he is also the size and shape of a seal. I look at him and I don't know whether to throw him a fish or to balance a beach ball on his nose.

Something had to be done. But of course, that was my opinion, not the cats'. My wife and I decided that the cats must diet. We came to that conclusion from the usual high moral plane of having just slimmed down ourselves. We have joined the Thin Church. So everybody in the family will join the Thin Church.

However, cats are like people in that deciding to go on a diet is merely the first step. The next step is deciding what kind of diet. That turns out to be a lot more limited than it is for people.

For instance, my wife and I took two very different approaches. She sought professional help; she paid sadists to starve her. So her diet involves an enormous amount of record keeping. Most diets involve a lot of vegetable chopping. Hers involves not only chopping but writing. She lost weight because, between the chopping and the writing, she never had time to eat.

My approach was different. While she paid others to abuse her. I practiced self-abuse and that can also be time consuming.

She finds it easier to diet with small portions of relatively normal and highly nutritious foods. I use huge portions of empty food. She eats tiny steaks. I eat boiled celery by the gallon. Different strokes for different folks. However, I am turning green and she isn't.

But there is no such variety available for cats. For instance, to my knowledge, there are no professional weight loss clinics for cats. There is no such thing as a chain of feline diet shops where cats buy cook books and weigh in every few days to the cheers and encouragement of fellow cats.

There is no place where a cat can go sit down with some pleasant, emaciated woman in power clothes and listen to her lecture on how the plan isn't just to take off all that cat flab but to keep it off for life.

And there is no place where a cat can go and buy a week's ration of prepackaged non-fat mice. There is no place where a cat can buy large cans of powdered sparrow to make filling blender milkshakes.

The hardest part is the exercise because any diet works better with some exercise. But what am I supposed to do, gather the cats in front of the television set each morning for 30 minutes of an aerobics tape?

And it wouldn't do any good to make them get down on all fours and do pushups. They are already down on all fours. Cats do pushups every time they kneel down to eat.

The diet options for fat cats are limited to diet cat food. And oddly enough, it turns out that diet cat food follows my approach to dieting. It is the empty-food diet. I reached for the 20-pound sack of the diet version of our cats' regular brand of food and almost threw it over my shoulder, it was so light. It turns out that it is about the same volume as the normal 20-pound sack but it actually weighs only 10 pounds. And you know what that means:

Cat celery.

They take regular cat food and whip it full of air in a blender. The cat eats as much volume as before. But it has half the calories. We are starving our cats to death and they don't even know it.

So I feel guilty. I feel so guilty that I fall asleep each night with my face in a bowl of chocolate chip cookies.

44. The Slobber Of Respect

It occurred to me the other day while watching one cat spit on another why it is that cats show humans so little respect:

We are constantly grooming them. So naturally, they assume that makes them dominant.

I used to watch young Sheldon groom Sterling, licking him behind the ears where it's tricky to reach, washing him in that disgusting way cats have—kind of spitting all over Sterling's head and licking off the dirt.

But the point is that it was always Sheldon, the younger cat, who groomed Sterling, the older cat. You never saw Sterling condescend to spit all over Sheldon's head.

This is obviously another instance in the animal kingdom of the lesser members of the pack or herd fawning over the dominant member, showing their subservience by picking lint off the lapels of the leader.

Cats, of course, aren't found in packs or herds. I am told that it is called a "clowder" of cats. The origins of that term are as fuzzy as the congregation it describes. And who knows where these terms come from—a pride of lions, a school of fish, a swindle of lawyers, a bore of professors, an overcharge of doctors, a wonderfulness of writers.

Webster's Third suggests that a clowder of cats may stem from a distortion over the centuries of the pronunciation of a "clutter" of cats. If so, my hat is off to the ancient wag who coined that one. It is appropriate, both in the tendency of cats to litter a house with kittens and in the way cats arrange themselves around the house. They tend to throw themselves down on the bed like a wrinkled shirt. They tend to clutter the room with their rumpled presence.

And at no time are they less dignified in their positions than while washing themselves—or while washing a dominant member of their clowder. But to be honest, I suppose they are not much different in that respect from a human being taking a bath. A human bather doesn't occupy a bathtub; she sprawls in it, often in the most disgraceful postures.

Cats are the same when bathing themselves or each other. The dominant cat will sprawl all over a bed, while the subservient member of the clowder anoints his head with spit.

And what an odd form of approval that is. I am grateful that those who take a liking to something I write merely send me kind letters.

On the other hand, the thought occurs that such rituals do take place in human society. We constantly criticize and revile our political leaders. We spit on them, so to speak. But in the process, we signal that they are dominant in our clowder.

We do much the same with cats. We pet them, smoothing their fur, behaving like their adoring constituents. We obediently scratch behind their ears. We behave like slaves, feeding them, grooming them, emptying their sandy little johns. We lick behind their ears in countless ways and then witlessly wonder why they show us so little respect.

They show us so little respect because we declare them dominant with our every action. To an animal from a culture where some are regarded as dominant and some as serfs, we say more to a cat than we intend when we lean over to scratch its ears.

Small wonder that a cat often acts in such a regal, disdainful manner. From his perspective, we are constantly declaring him king of the clowder.

45. Show Your Patriotism: Sleep With Somebody

I made the classic mistake of thinking they disliked each other just because they were always fighting.

Our 15-year-old cat, Delilah, went to that Great Fish Feed in the Sky last week. And I was surprised when Sterling, the surviving cat, spent the next few days wandering around the house yowling, apparently missing her.

I would not swear that it was ordinary grief. It may be that we had been slow to fill his food dish and he was fearful he would never see food again, which, in his case, would be a form of grief. The truth is that, if Sterling loves anything on this earth, it is a good meal.

Indeed, he used to clobber Delilah with regularity if she attempted to join him at the feeding dish during his two-hour evening snack. He is twice her size and would suddenly lunge at her with all his weight, throwing a body block and knocking her end over end. And if she didn't leave after that, he would chase her all over the house.

From all outward signs, she was no fonder of him. Sometimes, with no apparent provocation, she would reach out and swat him in the face as he walked by.

Fighting was their only communication, their only contact. They didn't sleep together, the way most cats will. And though it pains me to tell you, I fear Sterling is a racist. He used to snuggle up for warmth next to another part

Siamese, Sheldon. But he wouldn't sleep with Delilah and I suspect it was because she is nothing but a tabby.

Of course, cats don't sleep together merely out of affection. Cats can't afford blankets. So they use each other as blankets.

People do the same thing. You need more blankets if you sleep alone than you do if you share body heat. Thus sleeping together is not only friendly but economical.

Sleeping together also makes America less dependent on foreign oil, less likely to be victimized by some foreign despot, less likely to go to war. Those who sleep together are doing more for America than those who hog a bed all to themselves. So if you consider yourself any kind of patriot at all, you'll sleep with somebody tonight.

Most cats are patriots. But not Delilah and Sterling. Frankly, it was more his fault than hers. It was his monogamous Siamese streak popping out again. Siamese don't like to share people with another cat. And if forced to share, they become belligerent.

Nonetheless, Sterling, who never showed Delilah a moment's kindness, is suddenly showing signs of grief. He appears to be looking for her, mourning her absence. And now I am beginning to understand:

He and Delilah must have been one of those strange couples who show affection by fighting. I don't understand such people but we all know they exist. They yell and holler all day long. They lunge with words, throwing verbal body blocks into each other.

They snarl and hiss and quarrel for 50 years and more. People who get along better can't keep a marriage together but these fighters do.

In gentle moments, you can tell they like each other. Fighting is some unusual form of intimacy, some kind of rough love, some bizarre version of touching. They chase each other around the house all day. But they chase only each other. They wouldn't pummel anyone else. Nobody else is so much fun to fight with.

From a distance, their relationship looks exhausting. But it works for them so who am I to question? Nonetheless, they are a marvel. They give every indication to an outsider that they get on each other's nerves, that they irritate each other, that they drive each other up the wall, that they were cursed the day they met.

And then, when the inevitable day comes that one of them goes to That Great Fish Feed in the Sky, the survivor wanders through the house, yowling with grief, suddenly aware that the nastiest quarrel of all is the one you have with nobody, with nobody at all.

46. The Cat Whose Rear Legs Run Faster

The new kitten can run faster with his hind legs than with his front legs. That's a problem for a four-legged creature.

I turned on the coffee grinder and the beans clattered against the plastic grinding compartment with a rattle that would rouse the dead. Or the fuzzy.

It was the first time the 8-week-old kitten had ever heard such a horrible noise. First, he jumped straight in the air, feet already churning—just like cartoon cats.

Then, as his little feet finally found the floor, he began running. But his back feet were apparently more frightened than his front feet. The back ones caught up with the front ones and he was beside himself—literally; his hind end came up even with his front end and he was running sideways toward the door.

Worse, he was gaining on himself. His hind legs continued to run faster than his back legs, finally spinning him in a circle. He got ahead of himself. He lost his footing but skidded out the door, safe from that terrible sound.

But it isn't the coffee grinder that makes him nervous as a cat. It's cat nerves not coffee nerves. This little cat—Lyle—is new to our home so he is as jumpy as you would be if you were suddenly shipped off to a new pair of giants.

Lyle and his twin, Sydney, are our new half-Siamese kittens. They are replacements for the two cats we've lost in the last year. It is normal, after a decent interval, to replace them when they croak. So, the decent interval having passed, we are now keeping house, not merely for Sterling, the one cat who kindly didn't croak, but for these agreeable newcomers, Lyle and Sydney.

They are getting to know our house and its odd noises—especially sudden, loud noises like the coffee grinder. And they are adjusting. It's not that Lyle and Sydney mind noise. They don't. They come to us from a home they shared with a human girl. Every time we visited before bringing them home, the television set in that house was on, playing MTV, the rock video channel.

In my previous alliances with new kittens and puppies, I have resorted to alarm clocks to keep the baby from crying. If you have some fuzzy baby that is crying because it misses its mother, you are supposed to give it an alarm clock to sleep with. The theory is that the ticking will remind the baby of its mother's heart.

It seems to work. It seems to soothe small critters. But that's remarkable because the same device—an alarm clock—will make a grown man cry.

We didn't use the alarm clock with Lyle and Sydney. We did better than that. We used Lyle for Sydney and Sydney for Lyle. Each one's heart is familiar to the other. So they curl up together rather readily and drift off to sleep.

Especially if we treat them to the familiar sound of MTV. We leave MTV playing in the room where Lyle and Sydney sleep. And it works. They seem to find it especially difficult to remain awake during the rap songs. I have the same problem.

Soon the more common sounds in our home including the coffee grinder will become normal to them. Soon, they will be sleeping the usual 18 hours a day so popular with cats. Soon they will not even raise an eyebrow as the beans crash against the genuine plastic container. Coffee will no longer keep them awake. Or frighten them. And I suppose their front legs will eventually become as fit as their hind legs and they will run in the normal fashion with the front legs leading the way and the hind legs literally bringing up the rear.

They will also find they have a lot in common with a writer. We are also excitable. When the beans of fortune are crashing against the genuine plastic container of our existence, our mouths tend to run faster than our minds. We, too, tend to get ahead of ourselves.

47. The Baby Who Grows Far Older Than You

The time will come, as we live all the legendary ages of man, when we who were once little boys will become little boys again.

Similarly, the time will come when your puppy or your kitten or your small pet swine is far older than you.

And the time will come when the children we brought into the world become more our parents than we are theirs, when we reach the fragile age and they reach the bossy age and every conversation begins with, "Dad, you really ought to…" or "Mom, don't you really think you should…"

I expected that. But I never expected to be involved in a relationship where a baby I once looked after suddenly becomes far older than I.

I think that's what's happening with Sterling. He is about 9 years old. In human terms, that means he is becoming older than I am. Most of our pets live life in the fast lane, speeding from kitten to middle age to old age in little more than a decade. Sterling just went by me on the inside lane and he's pulling away fast.

That changes our relationship. We have been friends for several years. But our time together began with a lot of nonsense on his part. When he was a small kitten, he could sometimes be too wild and rowdy while I was trying to concentrate on serious matters. More than once, while I wrote, he leaped onto the computer keys, accidentally typing cat gibberish onto the screen. (But of course, some would say that's what I am doing now.)

As he grew up, he simmered down. These past couple of years have been a time when we have understood and appreciated each other more than ever because, for a brief time, he and I have been the same age.

We both see things pretty much the same way. For instance, we both get a kick out of the kittens up to a point. And we both get irritated with too much of their non-sense.

And now, as Sterling grows older at a faster rate than I and becomes more and more mature, there are times when he tires of my playfulness as well. There are times when he wishes I would stop running around the house like some brainless dog and just settle down on the couch and help him nap through the news.

As the days roll on—his faster than mine—I already seem too hyper, too childish, for him. And if I get too silly, he glares at me.

Where once he followed me up the hill and down the hill as I worked in the yard, more and more, he now finds a high rock in the sun and supervises my work from a greater distance in years as well as yards.

He reminds me these days of my father who puttered around the garden almost until the day he died but came to spend more and more time sitting in a lawn chair, smiling, nodding, supervising, watching the world go by and enjoying the view.

Sterling grows slow and mellow. The small kitten who once chased my shoelaces now chases memories in his mind.

Mind you, I don't pretend that Sterling or any other cat has much of a memory. But he has memories of a sort. People remember their childhood of years before. Sterling remembers today's lunch and that's about it. But he enjoys remembering today's lunch. And of course, as he grows more inactive, he tends to grow larger, partly because he always loved lunch more than most cats. Indeed, he has always loved lunch more than most hogs.

So the day will come when Sterling is not only older than I but bigger as well.

In fact, at the present rate, the day will come when I am stretched out watching football and he will climb onto the couch, drape himself over my legs as usual, and break my fibula in four places with the crushing load of his great girth.

But that's the risk you take when the kitten who once played with your shoelaces becomes an old cat who needs the warmth of a friend on the colder couch of his winter years.

48. A Matched Set Of Hairy House Wreckers

"I know what it's like to have two small boys in the house at the same time," she said as two teen-aged cats tore up the room, "so I don't know why I did that."

What she had done was to consciously, deliberately obtain two kittens at the same time—the only two kittens in the litter. Thus Lyle and Sydney are twins. But they are far from the first set in her family.

Well, that's not quite true. Michael and David, our sons, are 14 months apart. And my brother Bob and I were also 14 months apart. But to the world, when two boys are that close in age, they are twins. People see them chasing each other through the yard, wrestling together, knocking over lamps, tables and elderly relatives, and they can't tell them apart.

Even parents get them mixed up. To this day, when someone yells out the name Bob, I answer. For years, when Bob and I were growing up as virtual twins, whether an adult yelled one name or the other, we knew what it meant. It meant, "Hey you!" It meant, "Stop it!"

But the team doesn't have to be two males to be destructive. Our daughter and son were 15 months apart. And they did their share of knocking over furniture and pulling down the drapes. Two siblings near the same age playing together can do as much collective damage as five kids on their own.

As our two tumbling kittens now prove every day. They aren't quite as destructive as Michael and David who, at ages 4 and 5, obtained tools from the garage and took apart their own swing set. But Sydney and Lyle, knocking each other and occasional flower arrangements end over end, are a destructive duo, getting worse every day.

"I know what it's like to have two small boys in the house at the same time," she said again as the cats raced from room to room, looking for anything left standing. "I don't know why I got two of them."

Actually, she does know. She got two of them because she knows what it's like to have two small boys in the house at the same time. And she misses it—the sweet with the bitter, the vitality that invades your world when two kids, hairy or otherwise, race through the rooms of your life.

That's why we are pleased that both of our daughters are now expecting second children—children who will be close enough to be buddies with their siblings.

The Boise daughter who had a son three years ago is expecting another child next month. The Boston daughter who had a daughter a year ago is expecting again in May. And we are glad for them as well as for us because, while two is often too much of a good thing, one is not enough.

The initial impulse is to wish that the daughter with a boy might have a girl and that the daughter with a girl might have a son so that they could have one of each. Indeed, I have suggested, if they get it wrong and come up with two girls in Boston and two boys in Boise, that they swap babies, so I will have a variety of grandkids in each place.

But they regard the suggestion as strange. They intend, even if they get a matched set of boys in Boise and of girls in Boston, to live with the compounded destruction that will result when that sort of situation befalls a family.

I guess they know what they are doing. But the day will come when they will wonder why they ever brought two such creatures into the house at the same time.

Just as my wife now wonders why she was a double dipper when it came time to get a kitten.

But the day will also dawn for our daughters, in two or three decades, when a lonely silence will fall over their homes and they will no longer hear the noise of lamps falling and of vases crashing.

Before long the silence will hurt their ears. And they will bring a matched set of cats or dogs or grandchildren into their lives because they will remember fondly what it is like to have runty rowdies racing through the house taking the furniture apart.

49. When Do You Pull The Plug On A Friend?

I wasn't going to make any rash decisions about putting a pet to sleep because one of my sons was watching and I didn't want to set any ugly precedents.

Some day my children might be contemplating a similar fate for me so I was conscious of the object lesson in what I was doing.

The pet before me was Sterling, my failing feline friend sitting there on the stainless steel table of the vet for one more attempt to needle some vitality back into his old bones.

The question before me was whether enough was enough, whether the weakened life Sterling had left was better than the alternative. And such calls are often fuzzy.

But I said no. I said keep him alive.

I said that for two reasons:

1. While I was thinking on it, the cat looked straight up into my eyes with a "Don't snuff me!" look. And his eyes looked clear whether mine did or not. I decided there was still some life in there.

2. While I was thinking on it, one of our sons—perhaps assuming I was having trouble avoiding what would eventually have to be done—kind of encouraged me to go ahead if I thought I should.

Frankly, he seemed a little eager to settle the matter. I realized he might have to make a similar decision on me one day and I didn't want him to get in the habit of making snap decisions.

"Not yet," I said. "A person never wants to rush into a serious matter like this," I said. "You never know when some sick person will make a miraculous recovery and reward you with riches beyond calculation for saving him. Remember that," I said.

Actually, the decision was relatively easy in the case of the cat. True, Sterling is not his old self. He doesn't romp around the room. He has little energy. He doesn't eat much and he's a bag of bones.

But so far as I can tell, he is in no pain. He still snuggles up to my feet on the couch and helps me watch football. He still prefers the cat team, the Cincinnati Bengals. He still purrs, especially when they score.

But it is an odd thing to pick up a formerly fat cat and feel a furry feather in your hands. We constantly push food under his nose. But it doesn't often work. You can lead a cat to tuna but you can't make him chew.

We do have some thick obnoxious stuff in a tube and a method of sort of force feeding it. It's like dark peanut butter—mouse butter maybe—and we push it in his mouth. He sits there kind of gagging, trying to get it off the roof of his mouth, forced to eat it in the process, but obviously hating it.

And I hate doing it to him. I know it's for his own good. But it's like your old mother is fading away and doesn't want to eat. Would you hold her down with a knee on her chest and force peanut butter into her mouth? Sometimes it's a thin line between torture and dinner.

I guess the mouse butter helps. I know the pills do for a time. But one thing worked best of all—the sun.

This is a cat I remember as a kitten, playing in the sunlight coming through a winter window, chasing a walnut across the floor, making me laugh before I went off to work in the morning.

Just as we brought him back from the vet the other day, perhaps for the final time, the gray autumn clouds welcomed him home by letting the sun out to play with him again. A sunbeam streamed through the window and he strolled over to meet it there.

Cats love the sun more than anybody I know. They go outside on warm days—with a coat on —and sleep in the sun, sucking it in like fresh life, charging their batteries.

And it worked again the other day for Sterling. The sun seemed to inflate him with light. He sat a little taller. He grew a little larger. He sat there, head up, his eyes squinting with pleasure—in the manner of an aged man contemplating his life and wondering if he will see another summer in the sun.

He probably won't. He and I both know that.

But I was glad I hadn't been quick to end the matter in the vet's office. You can be so brave about putting a pet out of its misery that you put it out of its pleasure instead.

Besides, as I remind my children, Sterling may make a miraculous recovery and reward me with the riches of his friendship for having been the one to save his life.

❖   ❖   ❖

50. How Many Cats And Dogs Will We Live?

Sometimes we measure the lives of our children in pets.

For instance, we never fully realized that Steven had left home for good until his childhood cat died of old age.

When a kid leaves home for good, the seam between his kid years and his adult years is wide and blurry, an undeclared division. Nobody in the family announces or even stops to realize that a door has opened and a door has closed and a kid has escaped.

But when his childhood cat dies, and he has long since left home, you know.

If a person keeps cats and dogs throughout his life and each critter lives to an average age of seven or eight—given cars and ailments and fierce competitors in the wilds of the back yard—that means a person can measure his life in pets. If you have one pet at a time, I can tell you how long you will live:

You will live for 10 or 12 cats.

You will live for about a dozen dogs.

In our mind, Steven didn't become a man until Delilah died. He was still the kid—the baby of the family—who went away to college one day and would probably return.

I suppose Delilah sort of felt the same way, to the extent she did much thinking at all. She was not, as they say, a rocket scientist—though I wonder why they say that. Some rocket scientists are so narrow in their focus—so functionally stupid about life at large—that one might say they are no tabby cat when it comes to brains.

But brains were not what drew Steven to Delilah. It was love at first sight. As a half-grown boy he saw her at the city pound and declared that he would die if he didn't have that cat.

She was his final cat before leaving home, his final childhood pet. And she lasted longer than his childhood did. Thus when she died last year, it was the end of more than a long feline life. It was the official farewell to the last chick to leave the nest.

One day you have a kid and a cat.

Then you just have the cat.

And when the cat dies, you suddenly realize the kid is gone.

In his place is this man who sometimes comes home to visit. You realize your kid is one cat older and thus a kid no more.

Similarly, I felt a lot older when I heard that Hombre had died. Hombre was the dog our daughter Stacy, as a half-grown girl, spent night and day saving when his mother was killed by a car three days after Hombre was born. Thanks to her, Hombre lived to be 14 or 15 years old. And he's been gone several years now. That would tend to indicate that Stacy, my pup, is a mature woman. I turned my head for an instant and when I looked back, my little girl was another dog older.

I understand pets and parents better now. When I was 12, I acquired a cocker spaniel named Ginger. Thanks to Ginger, I spent the remaining years of my childhood with warm feet because that's where she slept until I left for college.

And then one year I came home from college and realized Ginger was blind. But she heard my voice, the friend who had left her behind, and came over and curled up on my feet.

A few months later, my mother told me on the phone that Ginger had died.

"Oh," I said, unable to say more without losing it.

"Oh," said Steven when we finally told him Delilah was gone.

"Oh," I said, each time I realized, through a pet death, that a child who used to live at our house was gone and had been replaced by an adult who sometimes comes to visit.

Today, the kids are all gone from home. In their place are the new kittens now romping through our home. I watch the kittens mature into adult cats and realize that a person can't live forever. It makes me wonder how many cats I have left to live.

Oh.

51. Why Do People Hang Around With Cats?

When you stop to think about it, it's odd that human beings develop such a deep bond of affection with dogs and cats. We don't have that much in common.

Ballerinas and truck drivers don't usually hang around together, nor do chemical engineers and newspaper writers. Yet they have far more in common with each other than they do with dogs or cats.

Nonetheless, people routinely develop deeper bonds of genuine affection with their pets than they do with all but a handful of their fellow human beings. Why is that?

The question came up last week when I lost the best cat I ever knew and felt the pain of his parting as keenly as I would a human friend. And that's odd. Though we both had hair on our faces and both enjoyed sleeping on the couch, we did not have a great deal in common. We aren't even the same kind of mammal. How could such a friendship ever bloom?

After all, in human relationships, we tend to pal around with people with whom we have something in common—people about as smart as we are, people who like the same hobbies we like, people who enjoy the same jokes we do, people who like us most of all because we are so much like them. There is a lot of self-flattery in our choice of human friends.

But look at my rather typical relationship with a cat: A cat has an I.Q. of about 3 and mine is at least 10 points higher.

A cat eats raw birds and mice and I refuse.

A cat is a squat little hairy thing that walks around outside in all kinds of weather on its hands and feet. It drinks out of a toilet. And it breeds in the bushes. No matter what you may have heard, I have done none of that.

So at first glance, a cat isn't the sort of person you would expect to become friends with, let alone develop a bond of affection that can be broken only with pain.

Nonetheless, if you see a man and his cat—a cat and his man—strolling across a yard together, you can plainly see the bond between them in their body language. You can see by the way the cat runs toward the man when he comes home—and from how glad the man is to see his pal—that these two widely diverse creatures are friends in the full sense of that word, not just in some master-pet arrangement.

And when the cat dies in one of these cross-species friendships, the grief is sharp and deep—so much so that, when my old pal Sterling died last week, I was filled with wonder at my own reaction. How could something so different take so big a bite out of my feelings with him when he went?

Part of it is that anything familiar that works out well is hard to part with, whether that is a car, a comfy old hat or your left arm.

But a car doesn't rub up against you. A hat doesn't come running when you get home. It doesn't lie on the couch with you and help you watch football.

And it doesn't talk to you. Sterling talked to me. I guess that's strange because I read a cat book one time that warned people against the talking of Siamese cats. It said they meow too much.

And they do. If you say a word to them, they will meow back—each time you do it. The cat hears you make an unintelligible sound and it makes an unintelligible sound back. It's a conversation with a cat and it always made me laugh.

I don't know what we talked about because he couldn't understand me and I couldn't understand him. But we talked daily without anything to say to each other at all. Strong relationships are like that. The talking matters more than what you say.

And it doesn't really matter much that you are different. Companionship doesn't require similarities. Affection doesn't require a lot in common, if it is generously given and honestly returned. Differences can be more charming than alarming if you open up your heart.

And so I now sit here with the pangs of his passing still fresh and I wonder, if that hairy little runt and I could get along together so well, then why can't the Irish and the English? Why can't the Jews and the Muslims? Why can't Republicans and Democrats?

We humans are the same species. It should be such an easy reach toward each other by comparison with Sterling and me.

I wonder about such things as I walk through the yard these mornings, feeling the weight of his sudden silence. I never understood a word Sterling meowed to me but that's what his friendship said.

❖ ❖ ❖

52. Epilogue

One lonely morning after Sheldon was gone and after Delilah was gone and not long after my old Pal Sterling was gone, I awoke to a meowing, accompanied by a rattling bedroom door. I sat up in bed on one elbow and peered toward the noise.

A furry arm was reaching into the room beneath the half inch of space under the door. This disembodied arm was feeling around, patting the carpet with its white-tipped paw, seeking something. The hairy mystery arm would occasionally hook the bottom of the door with that fat paw and shake the door, making a racket loud enough to rouse a writer. The sound was punctuated by occasional meows, as if the cat on the other end of that arm were yelling, "Hey! Wake up! Get out here!" I got up and opened the door.

There sat Lyle. Nearby was Sydney–next to their empty dish.

Their eyes said they were glad to see me. Their eyes said they liked me. Their eyes said they needed me.

Their eyes said life goes on.

I reached into the container for a cup of cat food and dumped it into their dish with a clatter of usefulness as satisfying to me as it was to them. It's a role you learn to love.

Once a cat butler, always a cat butler.

About the Author

Bill Hall, a syndicated Northwest humor columnist, is the editorial page editor emeritus of the Lewiston Tribune in Lewiston, Idaho. He has spent his adult life in the newspaper business with the exception of a year and a half among the big cats in Washington, D.C., as the national press secretary to Idaho Sen. Frank Church during Church's 1976 presidential campaign.

Three collections of Hall's columns have been published as books—"Killer Chicken," "Son of Killer Chicken," and "The Sandwich Man."

Washington State University Press published "Frank Church, D.C. and Me," Hall's humorous account of his time living in the wicked city of Washington while trying to escape from a presidential campaign.

Bill Hall is married to Dr. Sharon Taylor, a linguist and college administrator. Taylor is also known as a sculptor, both in bronze and in reshaping the uncivilized tendencies of two cats and one writer.

Hall and Taylor have six grown children, 12 grandchildren and more cats over the years than you can shake a mouse at.

#

Made in the USA